CREATIVE**ACOUSTIC** FINGERSTYLE GUITAR

Creative Techniques to Advance Your Fingerstyle Acoustic Guitar Playing

SIMON**PRATT**

FUNDAMENTAL**CHANGES**

Creative Acoustic Fingerstyle Guitar

Creative Techniques to Advance Your Fingerstyle Acoustic Guitar Playing

Published by **www.fundamental-changes.com**

ISBN: 978-1-78933-239-1

A huge thank you to all who made this book possible including Taylor Guitars, Matt Sears, Viv Pratt, Merissa Barcomb and James Davies.

www.fundamental-changes.com

Contents

Introduction

Welcome! This book is aimed at the intermediate-level player who loves acoustic fingerstyle and wants to go deeper into the multitude of ways in which you can approach this popular guitar style. Here you will find plenty of creative exercises that will enhance your fingerstyle technique and inspire new musical ideas.

The amount of content included in this book gives me great joy. Many of these specially written pieces are extremely personal to me and I couldn't have dreamt they would one day end up in book form. My hope is that the emotive, expressive sounds of these heartfelt pieces will be as inspirational for you to learn as they were for me to create.

The book starts off with practical, yet musical, ways to improve your fingerstyle dexterity and coordination. We'll then progress into more advanced techniques, with examples taken from a range of genres including blues, country and Latin-jazz. Next, you will be introduced to a wide variety of fingerstyle grooves and learn how to get the most out of a capo. This first half of the book is teaching you vital techniques you'll need later when you work on the some performance tunes.

The latter half of the book features some beautiful performance pieces to learn, such as *It's Not Over* and *Belle*. You'll be able to apply some of the skills you've learnt, before I move on to introduce you to Drop D tuning.

Take your time to work through each section and ensure you feel comfortable with the material in each chapter before you continue. It's not a race, so just enjoy making music!

The exercises featured in this book will work equally well on an acoustic or electric guitar, but the audio examples were recorded on a Taylor GS Mini acoustic guitar.

If possible, keep a video or audio practice journal, so you can clearly document your progress as you work your way through this book.

The audio for this book is available from **www.fundamental-changes.com/download-audio** and I recommend you download it right now. It will help you to hear exactly how each example should be played.

Finally, before we get started, I want to recommend three of my favourite fingerstyle pieces. I suggest that you take some time to listen to these before you dive into the first chapter. They set the flavour of what's to come:

- *Angelina* (Tommy Emmanuel)

- *Mombasa* (Tommy Emmanuel)

- *Grizzly Caterpillar* (Alan Gogoll)

Happy Playing!

Simon

Get the Audio

The audio files for this book are available to download for free from **www.fundamental-changes.com** and the link is in the top right corner of the site. Simply select this book title from the drop-down menu and follow the instructions to get the audio.

We recommend that you download the files directly to your computer, not to your tablet, and extract them there before adding them to your media library. You can then put them on your tablet, iPod or burn them to CD. There is a help PDF on the download page, and we provide technical support via the contact form.

Kindle / eReaders

To get the most out of this book, remember that you can double tap any image to enlarge it. Turn off 'column viewing' and hold your kindle in landscape mode.

For over 350 free guitar lessons with videos check out:

www.fundamental-changes.com

Join our free Facebook Community of Cool Musicians

www.facebook.com/groups/fundamentalguitar

Tag us for a share on Instagram: **FundamentalChanges**

A Brief Word About Fingerstyle Mechanics

Fingerstyle guitar technique means using the fingers and thumb of the fretting hand to pluck the strings rather than playing with a pick. Perfecting this technique relies heavily on learning to coordinate the fingers and training them to pick the correct strings in sequence.

This book uses the very common *pima* system below.

The thumb and fingers are assigned to specific strings and named using the letters *p, i, m* and *a*. This is inherited from classical guitar, so the names are in Spanish:

p = *pulgar* (thumb)

i = *indice* (index finger)

m = *medio* (middle finger)

a = *anular* (ring finger)

For each example in this book there is a letter written alongside each note to tell you which finger should be used. You'll notice that the pinkie finger has been left out, as it is not normally used in fingerstyle. If it does crop up in a piece of music, it will usually be labelled *c*. (The diagram below illustrates a right-handed player. If you are left-handed it is simply reversed).

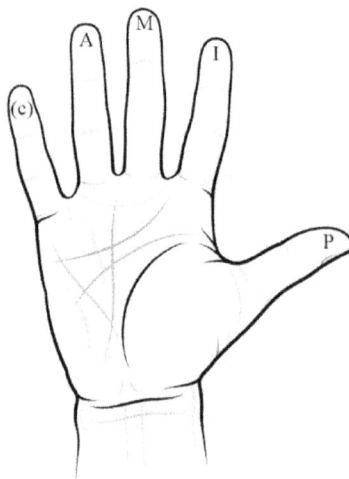

The thumb (*p*) normally plays the three lowest strings on the guitar (E, A and D); the index finger (*i*) will play the G string; the middle finger (*m*) will play the B string; and the ring finger (*a*) will play the high E string.

Checking your picking hand position

It's important to get the picking hand arm, wrist and fingers into the correct position so that you are relaxed, and the fingers are well placed to pluck the strings easily. Having the right position will ensure that each finger strikes its assigned string cleanly.

- Rest your forearm just below the elbow on the lower bout of the guitar body as illustrated below

- Allow your wrist to curve slightly, so you can touch the strings with your fingers

- Avoid anchoring your hand or fingers on the guitar body

Chapter One – Building Dexterity and Coordination

In this chapter, you're going to learn some musical exercises to help develop your fingerstyle dexterity and coordination – essential skills to progress in fingerstyle playing. This section may not seem as glamourous as later chapters that contain songs and grooves, but it will teach you the essential building blocks needed to develop solid fingerstyle technique, so you can comfortably play everything that follows.

All the exercises are in the key of G Major and build towards you playing an Afro-Cuban Caribbean style piece at the end of the chapter called *Limbo Limbo*.

Using a Metronome

Always use a metronome when developing your technique. Play each example with the metronome set at 50BPM (beats per minute) to begin with and ensure that every note you pick is clean and audible.

When you can play an example perfectly three times in a row at 50bpm, try raising the metronome to 53bpm. Continue to increase the speed in increments of 3bpm to a target speed of 80bpm+ (The examples in this chapter are recorded at 80bpm). This structured, incremental approach means you will only increase your speed once the lick is played accurately. I use the Tempo app (made by Frozen Ape) on my phone, as I know I will always have my phone with me. Then, I don't have an excuse to practice without a metronome!

Once you have your metronome set to 50bpm, it's time to start improving your dexterity. In this first example, pluck through an open G Major chord using the correct picking finger on each string.

Pick the E, A and D strings using your thumb, the G string with your index finger, the B string with your middle finger and the high E string with your ring finger. These directions are shown on the notation. As you pick each note, ensure that you don't accidentally hit any other strings in the process and aim to make each note a similar volume.

Example 1a

The next example uses a G Major barre chord and also introduces the "skip a string" technique. This is a fantastic warm-up exercise for the picking hand as well as a useful pattern you can apply when playing a chord progression. Pay close attention to which finger should be playing which string. It's much easier to lock in the pattern correctly now than to relearn it later.

Example 1b

The most popular fingerstyle picking patterns often use a repetitive *motif* (a repeating pattern). Example 1c illustrates this approach. This ascending pattern is a firm base for future examples. Practice it until you can play it without having to look at the book... or your fingers! You can use this pattern to play any 6th string chord shape.

Example 1c

The next idea is to play a high G note on every beat, while alternating every other note of a G Major chord underneath. This pattern starts out with some wide intervals, which create a piano-like sound. The challenge is getting used to playing two notes at a time using different fingerpicking combinations.

Example 1d

Now repeat the process using the B string for the constant pedal tone note.

Example 1e

The combination of using the thumb (*p*) and index finger (*i*) forms a major part of what is referred to as the *claw technique*. Think of two pincers moving together. Example 1f will help build the core foundation of this technique.

Example 1f

Imagine yourself in the gym adding extra weight into your workout – this is how Example 1g should feel. The extra weight will come in the form of using your middle (*m*) and pinkie fingers (*a*) on every pluck while alternating every other note of the G Major chord between your thumb (*p*) and index (*i*) fingers.

Example 1g

Moving on, Example 1h introduces the *four-finger grab* technique to combine thumb, index, middle and ring fingers simultaneously. If this exercise feels a bit uncomfortable, practise the thumb movement and the top three strings separately before combining them.

Example 1h

Example 1i is one of my favourite warm-up exercises for fingerstyle and combines all four of the picking fingers into a cool pattern that I'd use to accompany a vocalist. I like the wide separation between the bass notes and high notes. This intervallic space creates more interest than sequential string movements.

Much like working out in a gym, the fluidity, dexterity and coordination that results from regular practice improves over time. Practice these examples every day and monitor your progress using your metronome speed. It's also great to video your playing to spot errors and measure your improvement.

Example 1i

Triads

This next selection of technical workouts focuses on playing G Major triads (G B D) across a wide spectrum of the neck. Before you attempt them, spend some time studying the neck diagram below to get accustomed with their positions. The goal of the following exercises is to improve the coordination and interaction between both hands.

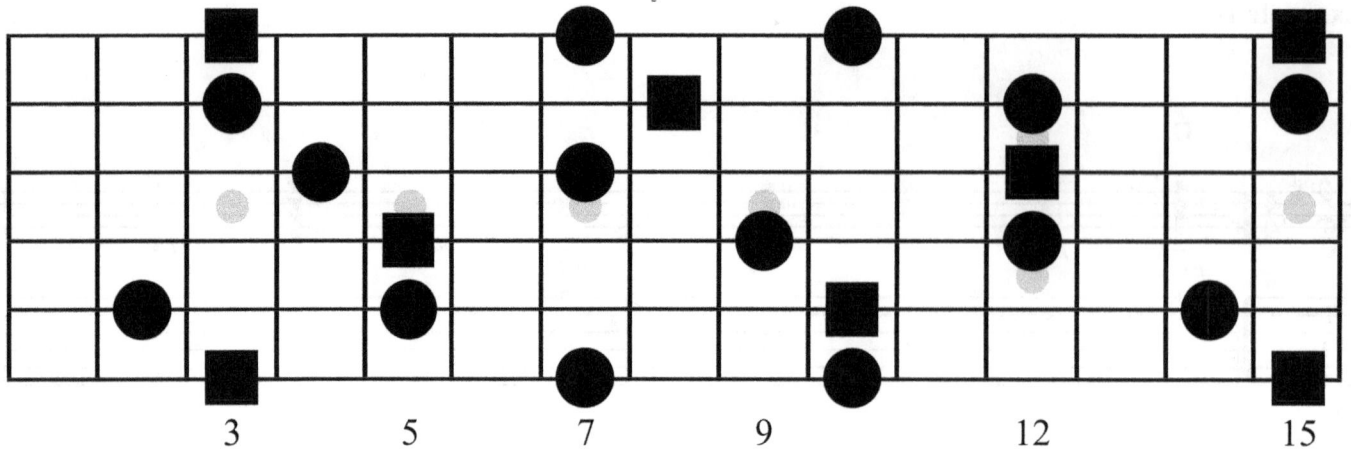

Example 1j uses G Major triads on the E, A and D strings. Use your thumb (*p*) to pick each note, moving it across three strings at a time. This technique may be new to you, but as you become familiar with it you'll see how the thumb gently rolls through the strings. Avoid digging your thumb in too deeply to help create that rolling or brushing movement.

Example 1j

Next we will concentrate on the G Major triads on the A, D and G strings using the thumb (*p*) and index finger (*i*).

Example 1k

In modern music it's common to play triad patterns arranged on the upper four strings of the guitar (D G B E). In Example 1l, use your thumb, index and middle fingers to play the three different G Major triad voicings on the D, G and B strings.

Example 1l

The final set of G Major triads is arranged on the G, B and E strings. Use the index, middle and ring fingers to pick them.

Example 1m

Now comes the fun part of combining different G Major triad voicings on the upper four strings. Patterns such as this are commonly found in African music, Reggae and Ska.

Example 1n

Although the next example may look tricky on first inspection, it is actually just the same four G Major triad voicings picked high, low then middle. The fluidity between the second beat and third beat of each bar may take a little practice to achieve, but after a while you will find yourself connecting the shapes with ease.

Example 1o

Now you're familiar with combining fingerpicking patterns, below are two examples that use major triads from different keys. Example 1p uses G Major (G B D) and C Major (C E G) triad shapes. The C Major triad shapes are shown in the neck diagram below for you to memorise.

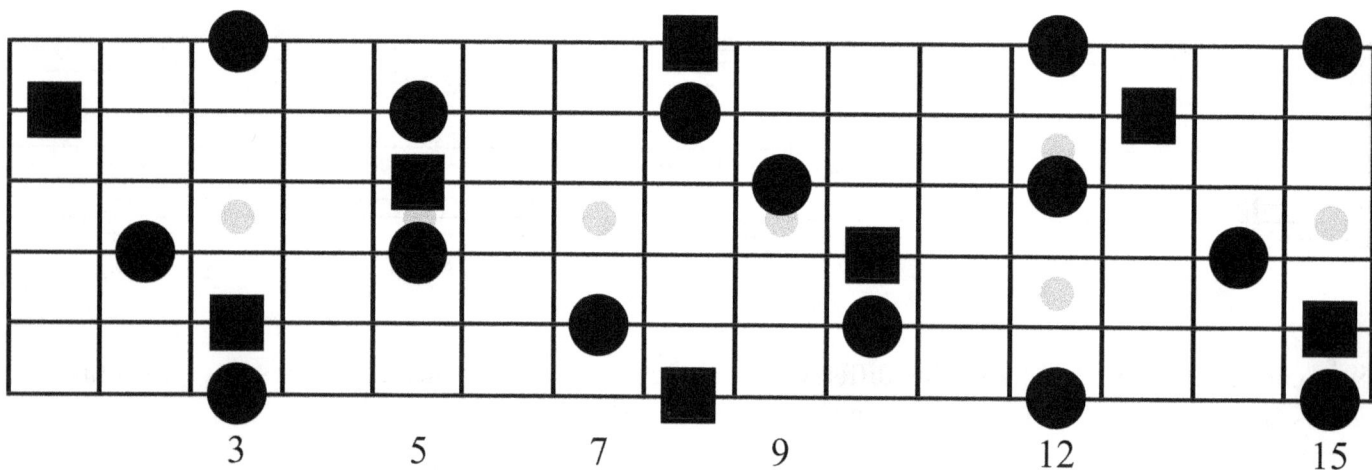

Example 1p

The final example adds a D Major triad (D F# A). The triad shapes are identical to those for C Major, moved up a whole step (two frets).

Example 1q

Musical Pieces

Technique on the guitar should always be learnt in relation to actual music. There's no point learning a technique just for the sake of it! Here are two pieces that focus on the triad shapes you've just learnt. The rhythms used create an Afro-Cuban vibe.

Before you play these pieces, listen to the audio examples a few times to get a clear idea of the rhythm and phrasing. Practice all the chords separately before adding the rhythms. As you get more familiar with the shapes, loop each bar individually before building up the piece, bar by bar. This process will help you to memorise the music and soon you'll be able to play the whole piece without looking at the book.

Example 1r

By adding double-stops (two-note chords) to the triad voicings you can increase the challenge of your workout. The perfect guitar workout should be built around your individual needs and ability level.

Example 1s

Chapter Two – More Advanced Fingerstyle Techniques

This chapter will introduce you to some fingerstyle techniques and riffs that will take your playing beyond the foundational folk patterns. These ideas come from Blues, Country and Latin-Jazz music and feature more challenging techniques.

Think of this chapter as building a new acoustic guitar toolkit. The more you use the tools, the more quickly they will integrate into your playing.

Claw Grabs

Earlier, we touched on some foundational exercises related to the three-finger *claw grab* technique – a popular sound in Pop, Jazz and RnB. Think of your picking hand as a kind of a relaxed claw. This position will help you play each string cleanly and fluently.

In Example 2a, use the thumb to pick the root notes on the E and A strings, and one finger to pick the third of each chord on the G, B and high E strings. I often use this technique when I want to play a light backing for a vocalist or in a two-guitar ensemble where the other guitarist is playing full chords.

Example 2a

Here's another example in the key of A Minor. You'll notice that the D string is played by the index finger instead of the thumb. You'll occasionally see patterns like this, which break the rule of using your thumb on the bass strings. Ultimately, it all comes down to what's the most comfortable way to play the music.

Example 2b

The Brushy Thumb

I like to call this next technique the *brushy thumb* and it's a great way to use your fingers to replicate the sound of strumming the guitar with a pick.

In Example 2c, fret the G Major chord and use the underside of your thumb to gently push through the strings in a similar motion to using a pick. Isolate the G Major, Cadd9, Em7 and D Major chords and practice the brushy thumb technique on each one before adding the upper two strings to each chord.

Example 2c

Banjo Rolls

A *roll* is a common technique on the banjo and describes playing a repetitive pattern on two or more strings, which when repeated forms a rolling finger movement.

One of the most popular banjo roll patterns in the key of G Major is demonstrated below. If the hammer-on patterns are a challenge, practice the picking pattern without them before adding them back in.

Example 2d

Example 2e extends the banjo roll into a four-bar pattern to create a common G Major country lick.

Example 2e

By moving the G Major banjo roll up the fretboard, you can create a C Major or D Major pattern. Changing fluidly between these shapes may take some practice and I recommend you focus on the fret you are aiming for before you move. If you train yourself to do this, your hands will start to follow suit and become far more accurate.

Example 2f

A fantastic technique builder is to apply the banjo roll to triad chord voicings. Example 2g demonstrates this idea using a G Major triad (G B D).

Example 2g

Harp-Like Scales

One thing that consistently amazes me about the guitar is that it can emulate so many different instruments, one of which is the harp. Creating harp-like scale ideas is a favourite technique of fingerstyle players because of their beautiful ringing textures. Although this technique is more popular with altered tunings, such as DADGAD, it is still possible to achieve it with standard tuning.

(If you want to learn more about DADGAD, check out my book *The Complete DADGAD Guitar Method.*

This example teaches you to play a G Major scale using open strings to create the harp-like effect. As well as creating a beautiful sound, this is a great way to break out of traditional box shape patterns. It only works in certain keys that contain notes on open strings, but you can always use a capo to play these ideas in any key.

Example 2h

Example 2i includes a natural harmonic played at the 12th fret of the G string and shows a different way to play a G Major scale using the harp effect.

To fret the natural harmonic, gently touch your finger over the upper edge of the 12th fret on the G string then pluck the string.

Example 2i

Alternating Bass Notes

A common way to adapt a fingerstyle pattern is to alternate the bass note between two strings (normally between the root and fifth or third of the scale). This idea is reminiscent of artists like Johnny Cash and Elvis Presley.

Example 2j takes a simple chord progression and adds a moving bass note pattern. Most of the chord shape stays held down throughout the entire bar and only the bass note changes. Make sure you're using the correct picking fingers, indicated in the notation.

I play the F chord by hooking my fretting hand thumb over the neck to grab the 1st fret of the low E string. This means I don't have to fret the full barre chord shape.

Example 2j

In the next example, the upper part of the picking pattern is slightly more intricate. Learn it by focusing on each two-note grouping. Repeat each beat until it feels comfortable, then move on to learning the next. Don't combine the beats together until each one feels confident on its own.

Example 2k

The following idea takes the alternating bass pattern around a twelve-bar blues containing dominant 7 chords. This is a longer idea using barre chords so take your time learning it.

Example 21

Percussive Elements

Adding a percussive slap to a fingerpicked chord progression adds a rhythmic texture to any chord sequence. To do this, gently tap the strings with the knuckles of your picking hand while keeping close to the strings, so you can immediately continue fingerpicking in the normal way.

The chord sequence for this example is AMaj, C#m7, Dmaj7, E7sus4 and E7. The fingerpicking pattern itself is the same in each bar. Begin by looping the muted slap sound until it feels comfortable. Then, learn the picking pattern and add the slap on beats two and four.

Example 2m

Example 2n is built around a jazzy Cm7, Abmaj7 and G7#5 chord progression and adds an interesting, muted pattern on the 2nd and 4th beats of each bar.

The first muted element is performed by relaxing the pressure of your fretting hand and picking the strings to create a percussive effect. The second element is the slap technique you learnt in the previous example. The third element is to once again relax each chord with your fretting hand but only pluck the root notes with your thumb.

The effect created by blending muted, fretting and picking hand mutes is well worth the practice time!

Example 2n

Latin Patterns

These Latin fingerstyle patterns will have you sounding like an experienced player in no time at all.

This first idea is a classic Bossa Nova pattern in D Major. I love using these Major 9 chords in Latin music, but you can play any chord quality you like. Listen to the audio track a few times to get the feel and the phrasing of this groove and ensure you use the notated fingering.

Example 2o

The next Bossa Nova pattern uses a rhythmic push where you play a chord on the "and" of the 4th beat of each bar. Before you play, count in *1 and 2 and 3 and 4 and*. The chord should be placed on that final "and".

Rhythm is the key to this genre, so spend time listening to how I perform each example before you play.

Example 2p

Here's the final Bossa Nova pattern in this chapter. Break down and study the rhythmic placement of the chords, so you understand this groove's foundations from both a technical and a rhythmic perspective. Remember to count *1 and 2 and 3 and 4 and* throughout.

Example 2q

The final two examples in this section have a Samba / Salsa groove and are great fun to play.

Rhythmically it is the use of rests (silence) that gives these grooves their unique characteristic, so pay attention to the ends of your notes, not just their beginnings!

The following triads and double-stops create a great guitar part that would complement another guitarist playing fuller barre chord shapes.

Example 2r

This final Samba style progression uses mainly double-stops in the key of E minor.

Example 2s

This chapter has been about opening your mind to some of the wonderful possibilities of creative fingerstyle technique and should serve as a jumping off point for you to explore new sounds and ideas. It is also a foundational building block for all the chapters to come, so feel free to camp out here for a while before moving on.

Chapter Three - From Technique to Performance

In this chapter we'll study the major components of arranging fingerstyle pieces for guitar.

I have separated this chapter into four sections: *basslines*, *melody*, *chords* and *fills*. These act as the fundamental building blocks of any fingerstyle arrangement. Let's briefly look at each element.

Basslines: These are usually played on the E, A or D strings and provide the rhythmic foundation and groove.

Melody: The focal point of most fingerstyle guitar should be the melody. You don't hum harmony! The melody will likely be played on the G, B or E strings, so it is at the top of the mix. When I am writing a piece from scratch, I will always begin with the melody and fit all the other elements of the piece around it. Also, you will notice that usually the melody note is the highest pitched note of any chord. Although not a hard and fast rule, this is often a good place to start in your own compositions.

Chords: Anything from two-note double-stops up to six-string barre chords can be used to fill out the harmony of a fingerstyle piece. I experiment with a variety of options before landing on the chords I use in a final composition. Experiment, and feel free to try out plenty of ideas.

Fills: Fills can act as a segue between sections of a song, or add a bit of a wow factor to your piece. Again, experimentation is crucial here. Fills should always be the icing on the cake, not the cake itself. Use them sparingly when there's a natural pause in the melody or rhythm.

Every progression in this book should be seen in terms of basslines, melodies, chords and fills

Although Example 3a looks easy, it shows you all of the parts that underpin the following example. Place your capo on the 3rd fret. You'll be playing the bassline movement, the melody and the chords consecutively. I love using ringing chords with a lot of open strings and this example shows three of my favourite open string voicings, along with a passing Ab/C chord (Ab Major with a C in the bass) that adds tension before resolving to C#m7.

Example 3a

Example 3b combines the previous three parts to create a four-bar progression with bassline, melody and chords all played together. I've also added percussive slap in bar one.

Example 3b

For the next piece I've written a Texas 12-bar Blues in E Major played with a shuffle feel. Check out the audio to hear how this should sound if you're unsure. I've taken a similar approach to the previous examples, where you'll first play the parts separately to get used to them, before combining them into one fingerstyle piece. Example 3c covers the bassline and the chords.

Example 3c

In this next example I demonstrate a cool blues lick to play over the A7 chord. I've given a suggested picking pattern, but you are free to play this one however feels most comfortable.

Example 3d

Now here's the full piece, but notice that there's no real melody. That's because this blues is a common rhythm guitar backing idea. It's the kind of thing you can use if you want to provide a solid accompaniment, but stay out of the way of a soloist. That said, do feel free to add your own embellishments.

Example 3e

The next piece features an alternating bassline that adds depth and texture to the fingerpicking pattern. All the alternating bass notes should be picked with your thumb and palm muted by gently touching the string with the underside of your hand right by the bridge. It's kind of like a soft karate chop position!

Example 3f

Often, you can change a bass note to create a whole new chord progression. Here, I have added a descending bassline of A, G, F#, F while retaining the upper part of the Am7 chord.

A slash chord is any chord that doesn't have the root note in the bass. For example, Am7/G means play an Am7 chord (A C E G), but with G as the bass note. For more information on slash chords, check out my video lesson here:

www.fundamental-changes.com/major-slash-chords-video-guitar-lesson

Example 3g

Example 3h is a fluid fill using the A Natural Minor scale. To learn it you should break it into bite-sized chunks of two-notes. The combination of slides and pull-offs give this lick a legato (smooth) feel. I used the *brushy thumb* technique to play the A minor chord in bar two, but you could fingerpick this as well.

Example 3h

Example 3i combines another bassline movement with an A minor chord to provide a rhythmic element to the single chord progression.

Example 3i

Example 3j is one of my favourite examples in the book and something I often use as a warm-up. The transition between the bend at the end of bar one into the bassline folk-fingerstyle pattern requires some dedicated practice, so work on the bend into the A minor chord until it feels natural. The other transition that may need attention is the FMaj7 in bar five.

Example 3j

You can begin a fingerstyle piece by writing a melody, a bassline, a chord sequence, or even a short phrase.

When creating a melody, I aim to make it memorable and I always ask myself, "Can I sing it back?"

The pieces I've written that have been the most popular are always the ones with the strongest melodies to draw people in. Often, to the frustration of friends, I get told, "I still sing that song you wrote years ago!" For me, that is the ultimate compliment and I urge you to play your songs to friends, especially non-musicians, and ask them which ones they prefer.

The next exercises are combined in Example 3p to create a longer fingerstyle song. Work your way through them methodically to get comfortable with each section before moving on to the whole piece. The opening bar of the next example has a somewhat classical sound and resembles the work of Johann Sebastian Bach. In particular, the combination of the A/C# resolving to D minor gives the music a distinctly classical flavour.

The run up of A, Bm7b5, A/C# to D minor is a finger twister and acts as a wonderful fretting hand warm up in itself, vastly helped by the fact that it also sounds great.

Example 3k

Next, the E7 chord here acts as a transition point to allow the piece to move to A minor. The A Blues (A C D Eb E G) lick in bar two leads into the Am7 chord that follows.

Example 3l

A fun way to move between two minor 7 chords that are a tone (two-frets) apart is to play another one in the middle. Example 3m shows this by playing an Am7, G#m7 and Gm7 chordal run as the opening phrase.

Example 3m

Another popular chord movement in classical music is to move diminished chords around in minor thirds (three frets up or down). Example 3n shows two diminished voicings, one from the root on the A string and one from the root on the D string. Experiment by moving each of these up and down the neck, three frets at a time.

Example 3n

This lick is reminiscent of the great virtuoso, Mateus Asato. The A Major scale is the foundation for this phrase and the combination of the single note melody with the double-stops is what gives it the Asato sound.

Example 3o

Now you are ready to put all the puzzle pieces together.

Example 3p

Bdim   **Ddim**   **Fdim**   **G#dim**   **A**

Once again drawing ideas from Mateus Asato, Example 3q breaks down the opening two-bars of the next full piece. Double-stops are the key technique used in this example and you will notice it features non-adjacent string double-stops (6ths) and adjacent string double-stops (3rds).

The lick starts off using the E Major scale before resolving to A Major. Put a capo on the second fret to complete this example along with the audio track.

Example 3q

E
Capo fret 2

A

This melody is based around the chord sequence A, E/G#, F#m7, Bm7, Esus4 and E and I recommend that you take some time to have fun with this progression. Pluck them as full chords, arpeggiate them, and get them into your memory before adding in all the fills shown in this example.

The A Major chord at the start of bar one must be played as a barre chord with your first finger so you can execute the A Major scale fills that follow. In bar two I have added the letters "S" and "P" to show where you *slap* the strings gently with your fretting hand and *pluck* the muted F#m7 chord for the P.

This progression is reminiscent of Tommy Emmanuel's music. I recommend that you spend a few hours on YouTube in awe of the mastery of this incredible acoustic guitarist.

Example 3r

The bridge section features a lovely movement from a Dmaj7 to D#/F. The melody line is played on the B and E strings while the chords add the fullness beneath it.

Some of the following examples look complicated on paper so I recommend the following strategy to learn them:

- Listen to the audio track a few times

- Learn the melody on its own

- Learn the chord voicings on their own

- Combine the chord voicings and melody without extras (such as the percussive mutes in this example)

- Learn the extra elements of a progression (fills, percussive elements and whatever else is included)

- Add in the extra elements to the chord voicings and melody

- Check to see if you are playing it correctly by re-listening to the audio track

Example 3s

Pull-offs and slides make this A Major scale fill sound quite fluid. Learn it slowly at around 60BPM and only increase the speed of the metronome when you can play it perfectly three times in a row.

Example 3t

This piece means a lot to me, so I have recorded it as a video piece. Use the link below to see the video:

https://www.fundamental-changes.com/creative-fingerstyle-videos/

Example 3u – You Got This

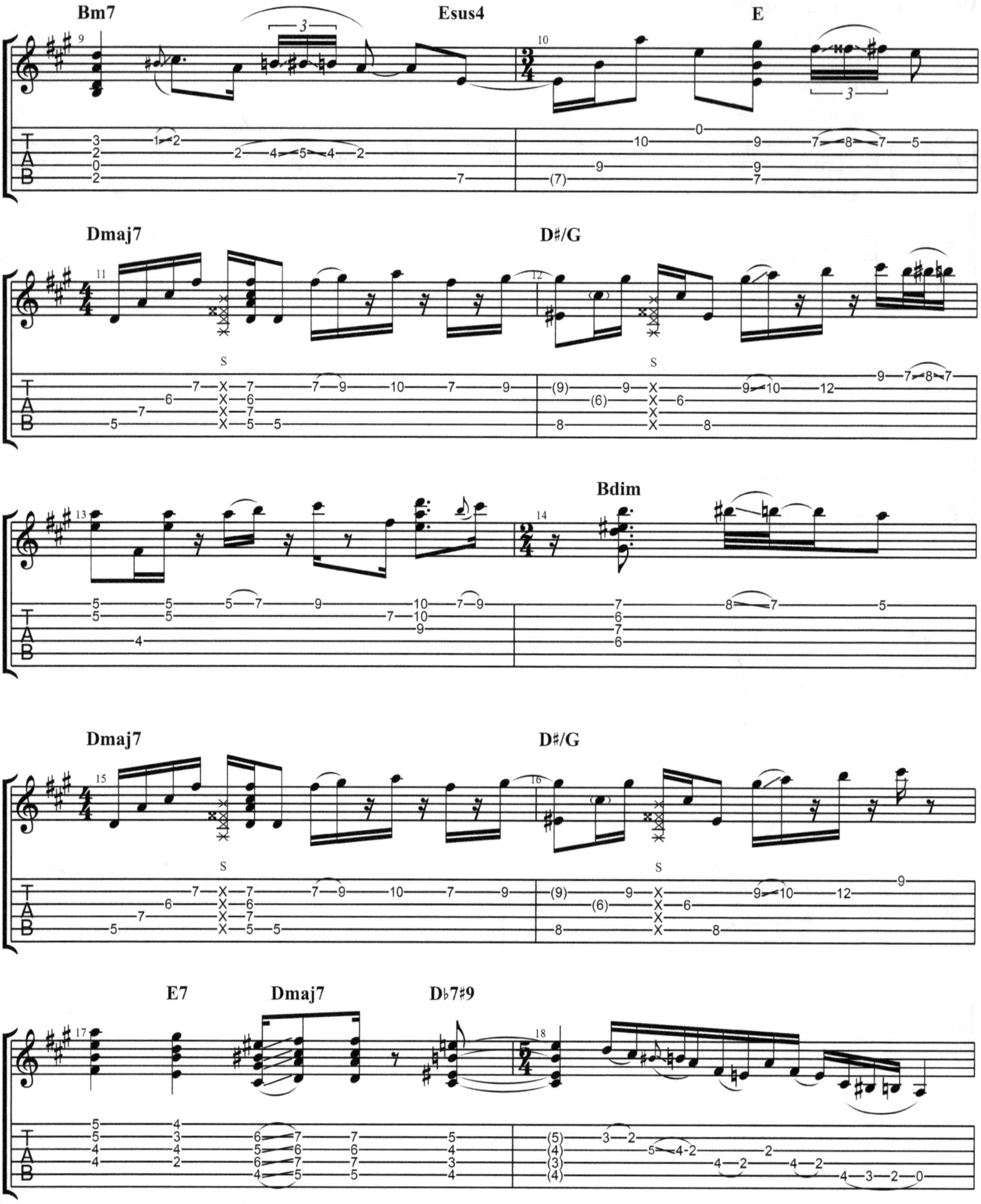
Bm7
Esus4
E
Dmaj7
D♯/G
Bdim
Dmaj7
D♯/G
E7
Dmaj7
D♭7♯9

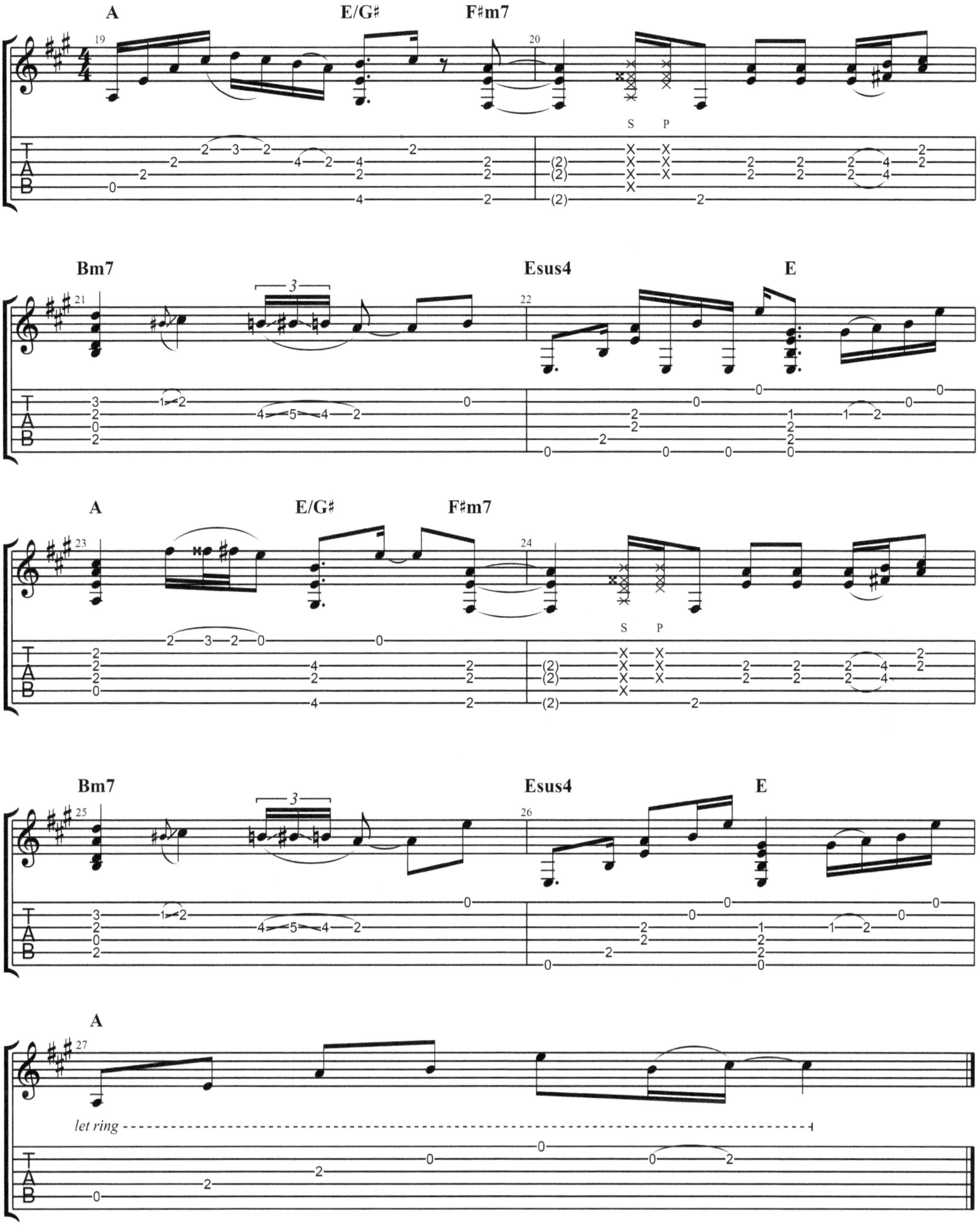
A
E/G♯
F♯m7
S P
Bm7
3
Esus4
E
A
E/G♯
F♯m7
S P
Bm7
3
Esus4
E
A
let ring

Chapter Four - Playing Grooves

One thing I have learnt about guitarists from many years of teaching, is that they often pick up a technique more quickly when it is placed in a groove. Sometimes learning full songs and pieces can be daunting but working with smaller grooves is an accessible and fun way to practice new techniques.

In this chapter, I have created a wide variety of fingerpicking grooves in different genres to demonstrate the versatility of this approach. I recommend playing through all the examples, then picking your favourites before committing them to memory. Use these as the basis for jamming with other musicians or as a starting point for writing your own songs and ideas.

Example 4a is a modern pop chord progression in the key of D Major, which include some Hendrix-inspired fills using the D Major Pentatonic scale between the chords. The technique introduced in this example is the use of percussive muted notes placed between the chords. To perform this technique, lighten the grip of your fretting hand on the strings so they are muted. Then, with your picking hand still in the fingerpicking position, gently slap the string with the knuckles.

Before you begin, investigate Jack Johnson's playing to hear this technique in almost all of his songs.

Example 4a

The next example is in the key of E minor and uses fills created from the E Natural Minor scale. Take note of the beautiful voicings of the Em, Dsus4 and C5 chords that make a nice change from the standard shapes. Once again, add rhythmic slaps between the Dsus4 and C5 chord shapes to add a percussive element to the groove.

This groove also introduces slides that add life to your fills.

Example 4b

Major 7, Minor 7 and Dominant 7th chords work beautifully when used in conjunction with fingerstyle acoustic guitar technique. After you have completed this example, learn some jazz standards, such as *Autumn Leaves*, to further your repertoire.

Example 4c

Example 4d has a bluesy country feel and is in the key of A. It uses double-stops and has a syncopated groove. You may find it easier to practice this example without the percussive mutes at first, to get used to alternating between the root notes and the double-stops before adding them back in.

Example 4d

I love chords with open strings that ring into each other. For that reason, Example 4e is one of my favourite grooves in this chapter. It's also a great backing track to play solos over. This example is in the key of E Major.

Example 4e

A mixture of arpeggiating and plucking multiple strings together is a great way to build strong fingerpicking patterns. This example in the key of E Major shows more voicings that have ringing open strings. The fill at the end of bar four is from the E Major scale and includes the chromatic note G to create a bluesy sound.

Example 4f

Fingerpicking also works great in a funkier context as shown in this G Minor groove. The fills at the end of bars two and four are a combination of the G Blues scale and the G Natural Minor scale.

Example 4g

Example 4h will probably introduce at least one new chord shape to you. Before you dive into the fingerpicking patterns and fills in this groove, I highly recommend you fret the full chord shapes and practice moving between shapes.

Like the previous example, this idea is also in the key of G Minor, with a fill in bar two from the G Natural Minor scale.

Example 4h

Fingerpicking blended with chords that feature open strings is a great musical combination. The key of E is a good key for creating chord progressions on the guitar, as you can let the high B and E strings ring out as you move through a variety of chord shapes.

Example 4i

Only one thing beats jamming on a 12-bar blues: having an awesome fingerpicked groove to add to the traditional 12-bar pattern! This is one of the most common progressions used at jam nights and here is a fun groove to throw out there.

As well as practicing Example 4j in the key of A as written, I recommend moving it to as many keys as possible. Other popular keys to jam in are Bb and Eb.

Example 4j

When learning fingerpicking patterns, it's important to spend time playing in different time signatures. Example 4k is in 12/8, which means all the notes have a triplet feel. I use the word "el-e-phant" to count triplets with my students, but any three-syllable word will work.

This groove has a similar progression to the Gary Moore's *Parisienne Walkways*.

Example 4k

As I wrote this book, I spent a lot of time listening to the Eric Clapton album *Unplugged,* which I highly recommend you listen to and steal as many of Clapton's fingerpicking treats as possible!

Example 4l is inspired by the piece *Signe* from *Unplugged* and uses some cool slash chord voicings in the key of E Major.

For more information on slash chords check out this video lesson:

www.fundamental-changes.com/major-slash-chords-video-guitar-lesson

Example 4l

Example 4m has a classical feel created by the use of diminished chord shapes and the resolution from F to E in bar four.

After you have learnt this example, check out the tune *Tears in the Rain* by Joe Satriani.

Example 4m

D minor is known as the saddest of all keys. That feeling can be intensified by fingerpicking the chord progression and allowing each note to ring out separately. I like this opening G minor voicing, especially when it resolves to the A Major chord in bar four.

Example 4n

I love using 6th intervals in my playing and Example 4p is based on the John Mayer smash hit *Slow Dancing in a Burning Room*. Playing 6ths works particularly well with fingerpicking as there is often a string skip involved which is hard to play with a pick.

This example is in the key of E Minor and uses the E Natural Minor scale to highlight the changes between the chords.

Example 40

Picture this, Jimi Hendrix is on a day off from touring and he is sat in his apartment with an acoustic guitar. He wants to write a 12-bar pattern for an upcoming song he is working on, but decides to fingerpick it. This is the idea I had when writing this example.

I used the E Blues scale to create fills and the introductory melodic "call". The "response" is the chord pattern in the bar that follows it. This 12-bar Blues pattern is super fun to play and looks impressive too when played at a quicker tempo.

Example 4p

Fifteen-year-old me sat down by a river in France once and wrote this piece called *La Rivera*. Admittedly, I still do not know why the title was in Spanish, but that somehow adds to it. My concept here was to take the barre chord shapes I know, but not play the barre and leave the strings that the barre would fret as open strings. Example 4q is the result of that experiment – one that holds fond memories to this day.

Example 4q

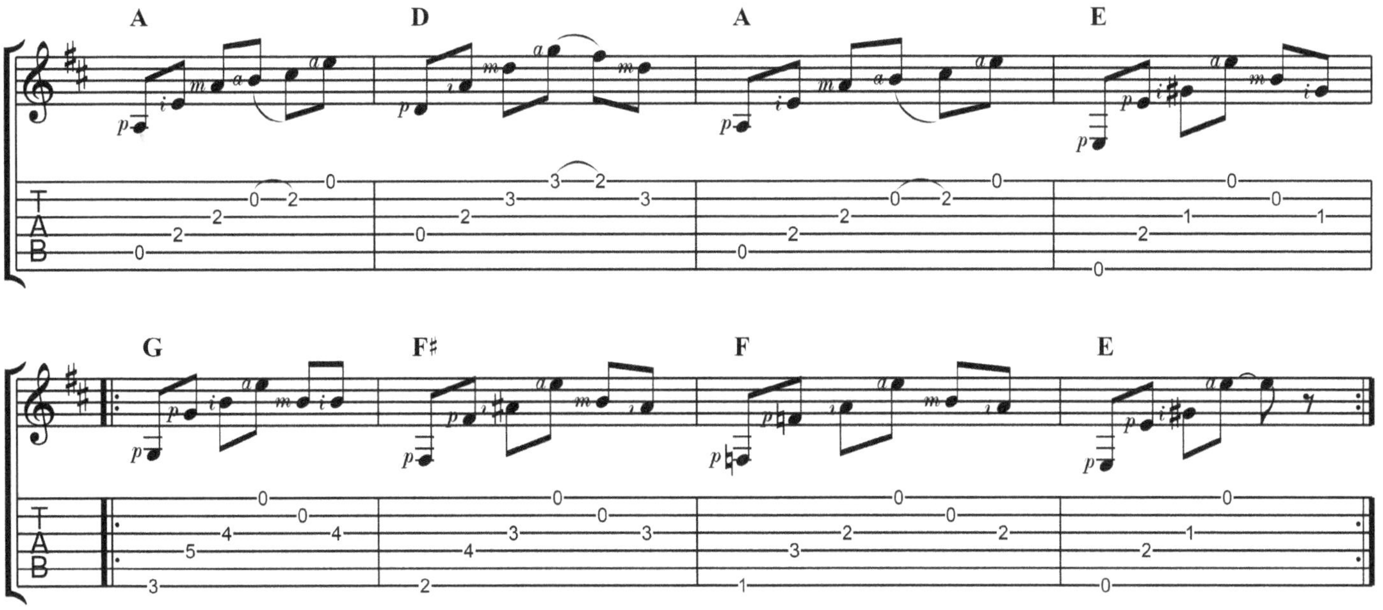
A
D
A
E
G
F♯
F
E
TAB

Chapter Five - Downtime

When I was growing up, my father wrote a piece called *Downtime*. It was a huge hit in our house and I would hear my dad play its main phrases night after night when he was home from one of his overseas jobs. So, in this book, I wanted to honour the person who inspired me to play by including a piece he wrote.

Downtime is in E Major and uses fragments from that scale throughout the entire piece.

This piece relies heavily on triplets and is notated in 12/8 for simplicity. The rhythm is percussive and funky and includes percussive muted slaps with your fretting hand. If you need a refresher on how to perform these muted slaps refer back to Chapter Two.

Minor 7th voicings are featured throughout and the breakdown includes an even wider variety of jazz chords while the melody line is played on the B and E strings. You may find it helpful to practice the melody line and the chord voicings separately before joining them together.

At the end of *Downtime* is a Neo-Soul style chordal run using the E Major scale that ends with a combination of 6/9 and Major 7 chords. I have included fretboard diagrams for these below.

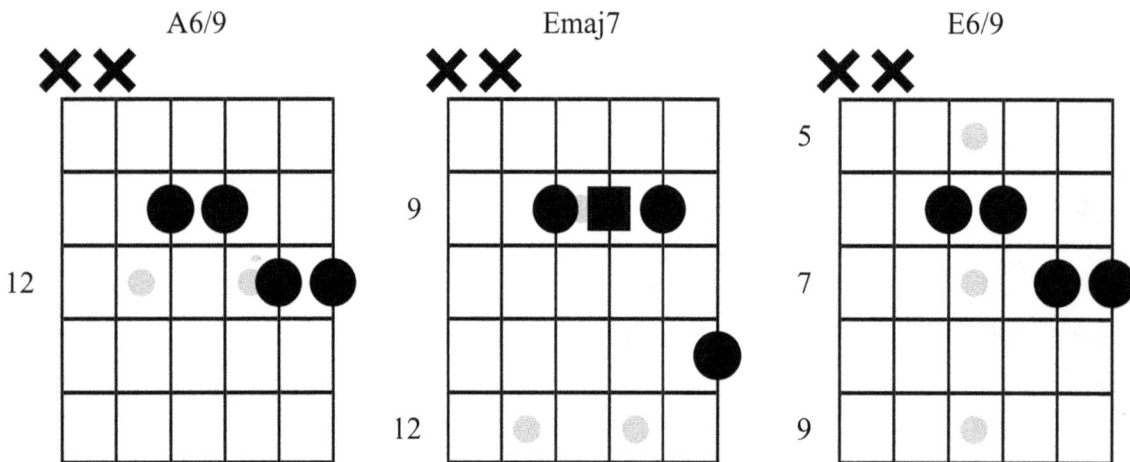

I've recorded a video performance of *Downtime,* so watch this before learning the entire piece. The full video can be seen here:

https://www.fundamental-changes.com/creative-fingerstyle-videos/

I am proud to share this piece as it was the soundtrack of my childhood. Some of my earliest memories of his guitar playing are dear to my heart. This one is for you, Dad!

Example 5a

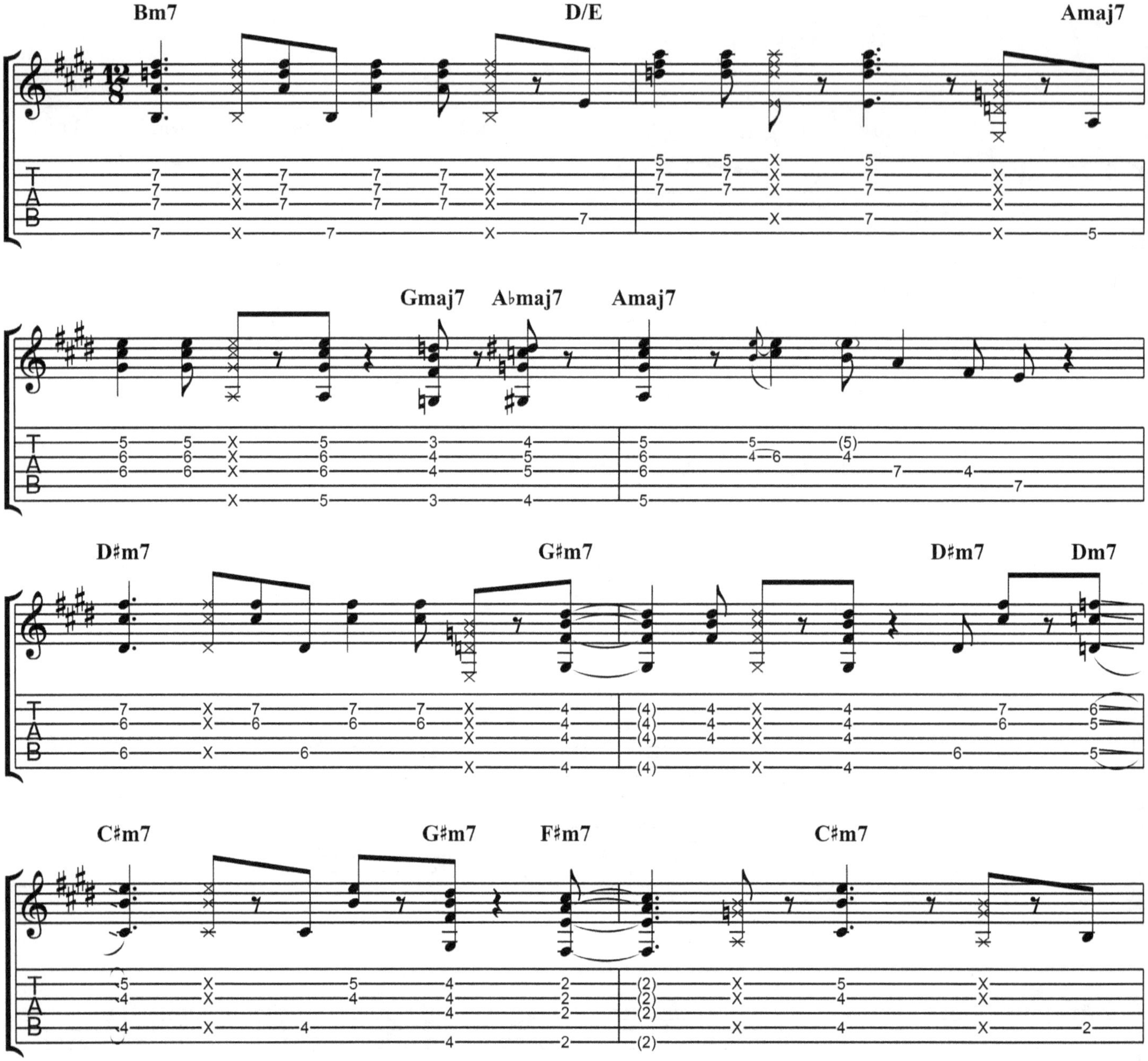
Bm7
D/E
Amaj7
TAB
Gmaj7
A♭maj7
Amaj7
TAB
D♯m7
G♯m7
D♯m7
Dm7
TAB
C♯m7
G♯m7
F♯m7
C♯m7
TAB

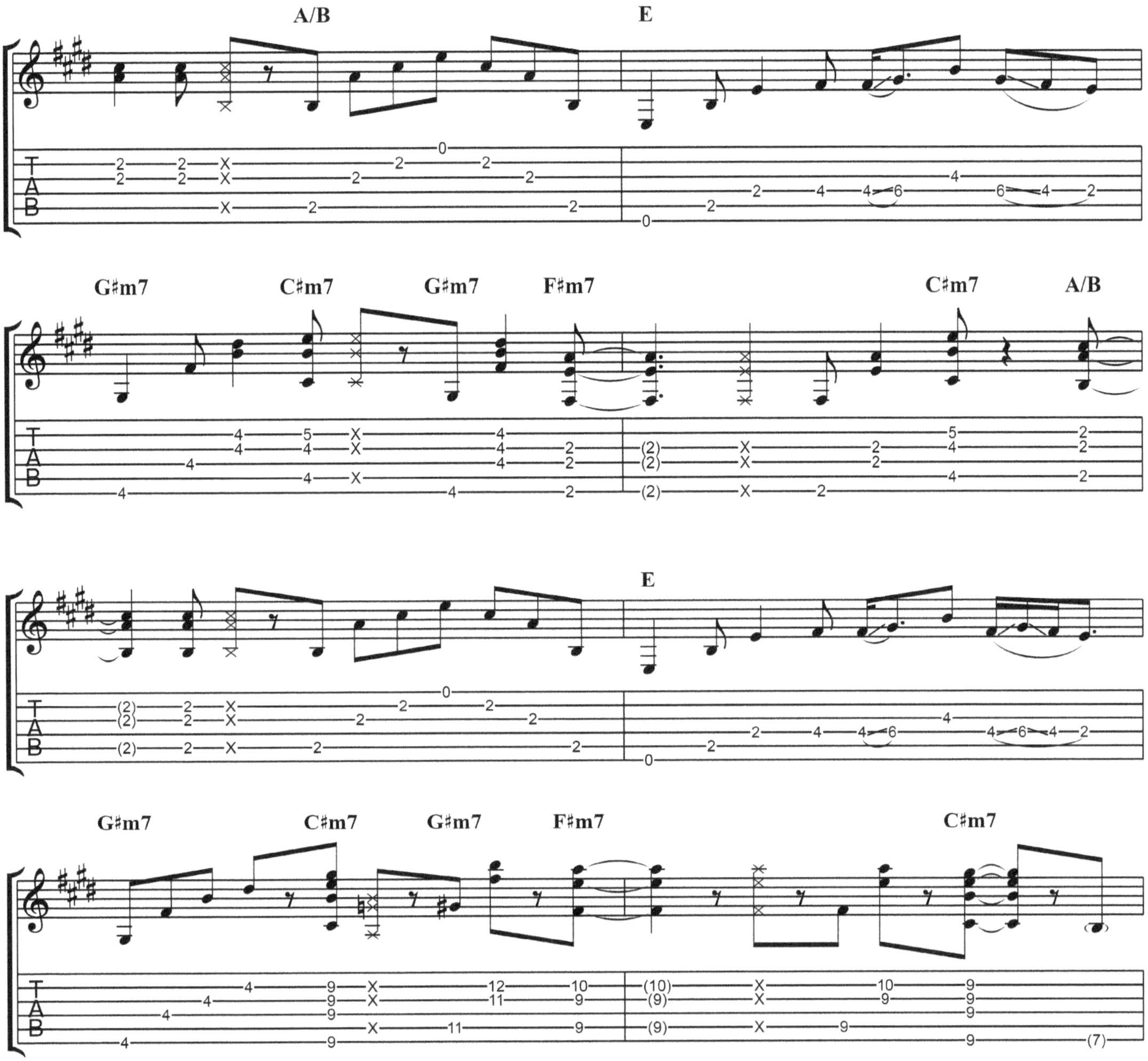

2/5

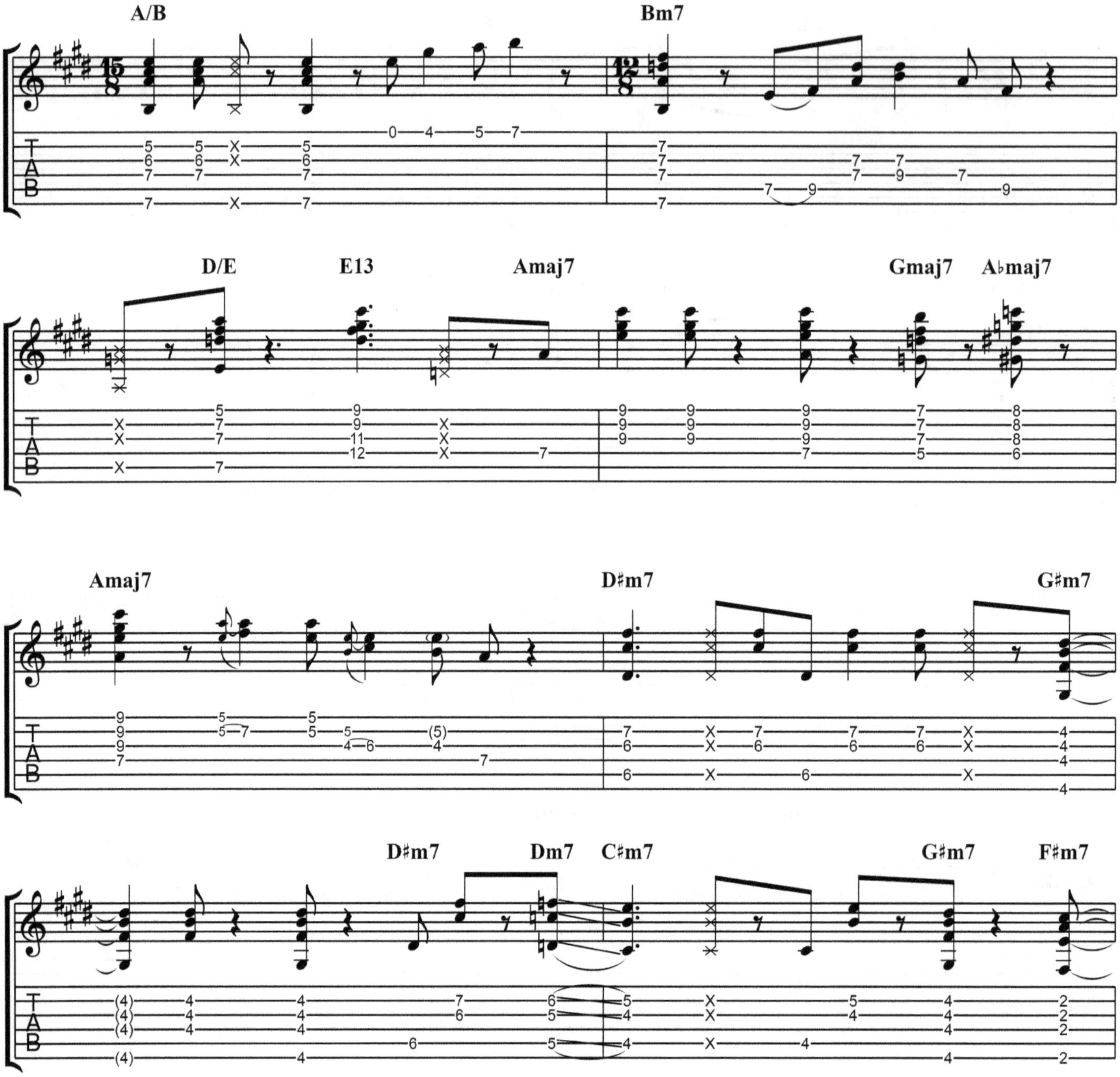
A/B
Bm7
D/E
E13
Amaj7
Gmaj7
A♭maj7
Amaj7
D♯m7
G♯m7
D♯m7
Dm7
C♯m7
G♯m7
F♯m7

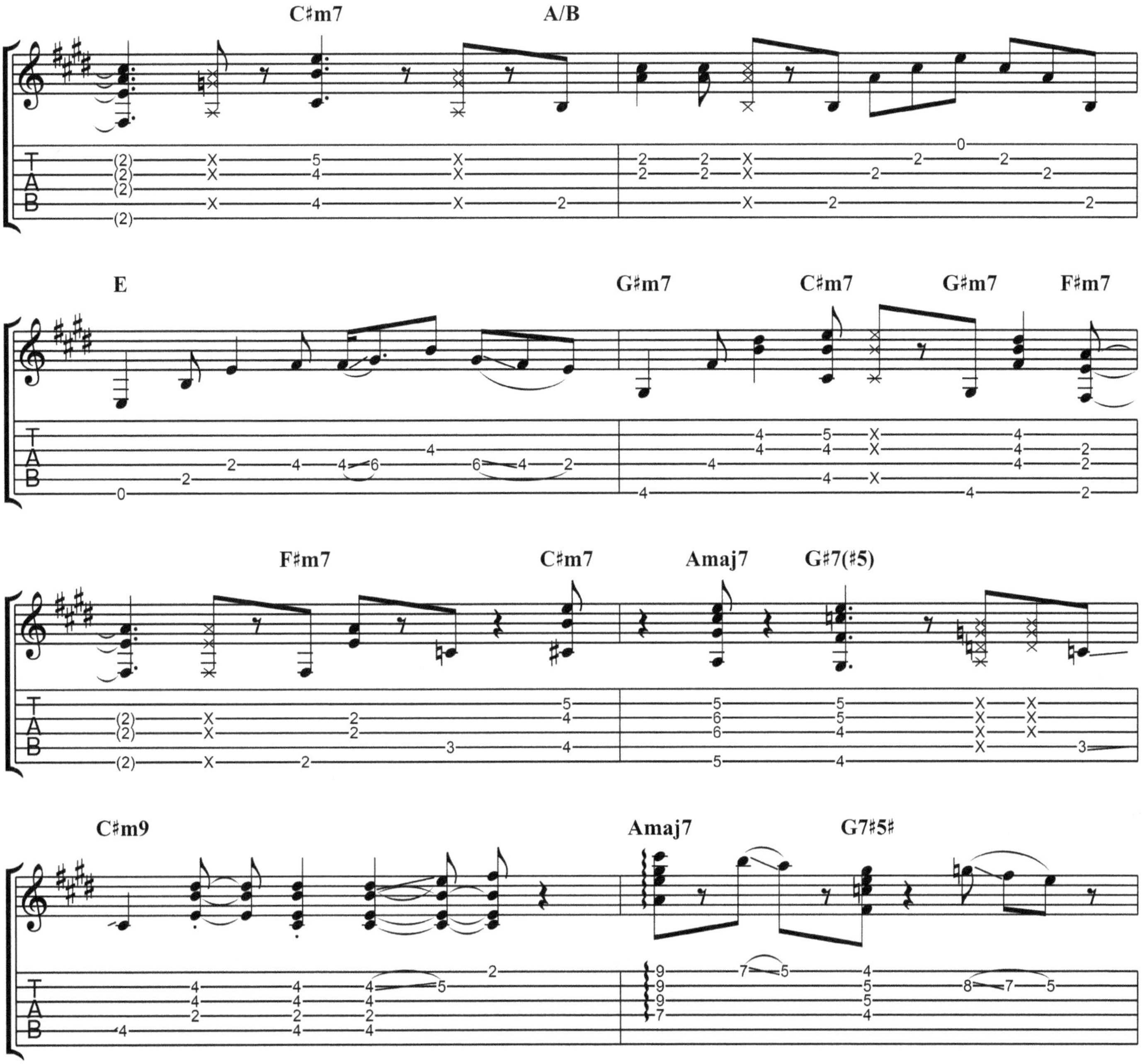
C♯m7
A/B
E
G♯m7
C♯m7
G♯m7
F♯m7
F♯m7
C♯m7
Amaj7
G♯7(♯5)
C♯m9
Amaj7
G7♯5♯

C♯m11
G♯/C
A13
G♯7(♯5)
C♯m9
Amaj7
G♯7♯5
C♯m11
G♯/C
Emaj7/G♯
A6
A/B
E
G♯m7
C♯m7
G♯m7
F♯m7
C♯m7
A/B

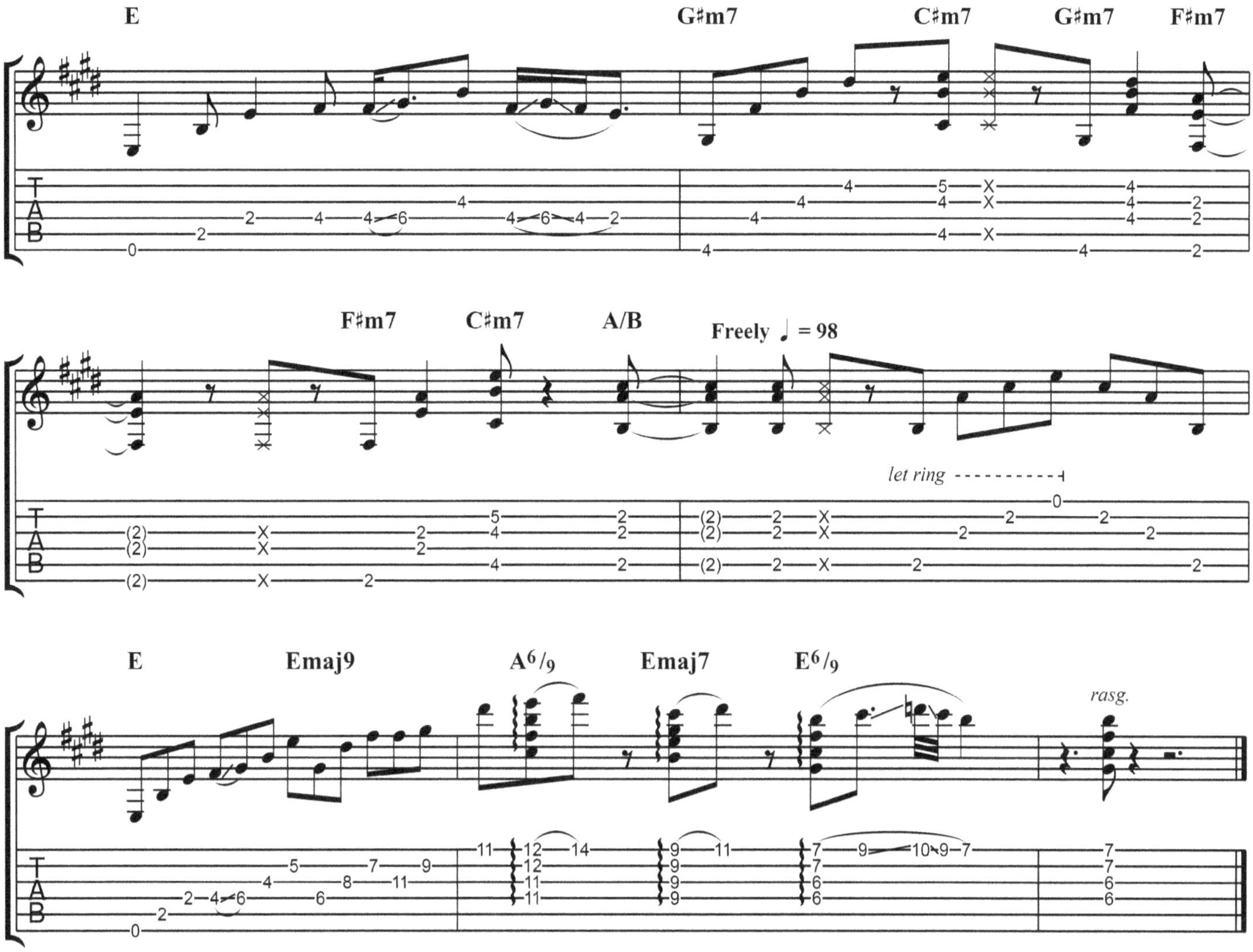
E
G♯m7
C♯m7
G♯m7
F♯m7
F♯m7
C♯m7
A/B
Freely ♩ = 98
let ring
E
Emaj9
A6/9
Emaj7
E6/9
rasg.

Chapter Six - Using A Capo

This chapter introduces one of my favourite subject areas: using a capo. When it comes to seeing what a capo can do, there's probably no better place to start than studying Tommy Emmanuel, who has been a huge source of inspiration in writing this book. Have a listen to his masterpiece *Angelina*, which he wrote for his daughter, and look out for the capo.

I particularly enjoy using a capo when writing an instrumental fingerstyle piece and playing in a duet with a vocalist.

Why Use a Capo?

The major advantage of using a capo is to play open chord shapes around the fretboard. It means you can use those chords in keys where they would normally be unobtainable. In this chapter I have used a capo to play fundamental chord progressions in ways that would be impossible due to the stretches involved.

What Capo Should I Buy?

I personally have always used Kyser Capo's but most capos that cost more than $20 should produce decent results.

Placing the Capo on the Guitar

Ensure you put the capo on the correct way around by placing the clip nearest to the bass E string. Place the capo roughly in the middle of the frets and make sure you don't over tighten it.

The first set of chord sequences in this chapter follow the chord progression C, G, Am and F.

Example 6a shows how to fret the open chord voicings of C, G, Am and F without a capo. I have opted for the non-barre version of F Major and used my thumb to fret the 6th string note. This leaves the 4th finger free to play additional melody notes around the shape, as you'll see in the next example.

Example 6a

Adding C Major scale fills to the chord sequence pads out the sound and creates interest. Example 6b uses a *call and response* structure where the first half of the bar is the call, and the second half is the response. Although I use these fills extensively, try not to add too many of them if you are playing a rhythm guitar part in a band as it can get quite distracting in the music.

Example 6b

Now I'll play the same chord sequence in different parts of the neck by placing the capo at different frets. Place the capo at the 3rd fret and play the chord shapes of A, E, F#m and D. Next, I add a nice melodic fingerstyle pattern around these chords. Barre your first finger when playing the A Major chord at the start of bar one to make the melody line much easier to play.

Example 6c

Move the capo up to the 5th fret and play the chord shapes of G, D, Em and C to create the same chord progression (C G Am F). Even though the actual chord progression is identical, where I place the capo can dramatically change the feel of how the chords flow together.

Learn this example in four chunks, around each chord shape.

Now fret the G shape leaving the high E string open and use your first finger to play both hammer-ons. As you reach the top of this G shape you will need to fret a Dsus4 shape before descending with a fill around the D chord. For the E minor shape in bar two, I once again use my first finger to play the hammer-on patterns before descending down around the fretted C shape.

Example 6d

To play the C, G, Am, F chord sequence higher up the neck, apply a capo at the 7th fret and play the shapes of F, C, Dm and Bb. For the F shape use your thumb over the top of the neck to play the 6th string, making it easier to access the open 3rd string.

Keep in mind that the fills are just suggestions, so please use them as a base for your own ideas. The simplest way to add some variation is to play the fill bars in a different order. Experiment and create your own chord progressions!

Example 6e

Now place your capo on the eighth fret and play these E, B, open C# minor and A shapes. Example 6f is a popular pop fingerpicking pattern that uses an off-beat rhythm.

Example 6f

Now we'll use the D, A, B minor and G shapes to create the same chord sequence.

Barre the A shape in the second half of bar one with your first finger to allow easier access to the third fret of the B string. The B minor shape in bar two requires a bit of finger independence as all the fingers of your fretting hand are used. I have shown in the notation how I play this shape, and although it's a bit fiddly, the result is well worth the effort.

Example 6g

Now that you have moved the chord sequence of C, G, A minor and F all around the neck using a capo we will apply the same strategy to a different chord sequence. By the end of this chapter you will see hundreds of new opportunities to use open chord sequences in new creative ways. This is a fantastic benefit to both your rhythm guitar playing and your musical process when writing your next song. You can apply this strategy to almost any open chord sequence, so keep that in mind as you progress through the rest of this chapter and see if you can find new ways to play the examples.

The chord sequence used for the next examples is F, D Minor, C and Bb. Example 6h shows the basic chord voicings for this progression near the nut. You will notice that the F chord is a barre shape, but as you move the sequence around the neck with a capo you can use open chord voicings for it instead.

Example 6h

Fingerstyle playing is endlessly creative because you can play any chord as just one well-placed note, or up to five notes at once if add your pinkie when picking. I've played the F, D minor, C and Bb pattern with a folk fingerstyle pattern, then embellished it with a pull-off on the D minor shape and a hammer-on on the C shape.

Example 6i

Playing barre chords for a long time is strenuous on the hands and can leave them tired and worn out. This is especially true in singer-songwriter settings, or when you are in a vocal guitar duo. The "life hack" is to use a capo so that the chords you would have to play as barre chords can now be played as open chords.

Example 6j shows the F, D minor, C and Bb chord sequence played with a capo at the 3rd fret, so the shapes can be played as D, B minor (as an open voicing), A and G. It common to play the root notes of a fingerstyle pattern first, but Example 6j turns that on its head by picking the upper part of each chord before the root note.

Example 6j

Next, place your capo on the 5th fret and play the C, A minor, G and F shapes. Listen to the audio track and follow along with the music before playing anything, as it's certainly more intuitive to hear this one rather than read it. Notice how the hammer-ons are the foundational element of how the sequence is constructed. Start off small, learning one or two beats at a time, before joining them together into the full sequence. Play the F shape with your thumb on the 6th string, to allow the access to the hammer-on.

Example 6k

Now place your capo at the eighth fret and play the A, F# minor, E and D shapes to create the same chord sequence. The next example shows that you don't have to play all the notes of each chord at once, especially when there are barre chords involved.

Example 6l

F   Dm   C   B♭

Capo fret 8

Place the capo on the tenth fret and play the open chord shapes of G, E minor, D and C. This example has a distinctly folk tonality that's created by playing plucked chords high up the neck with a repeating melodic pattern on the top strings. Make the pull-offs as dynamically even as possible. You may want to isolate those patterns and practice them separately before adding them into the full sequence.

Example 6m

C

Capo fret 5

The final examples in this chapter work towards you playing the piece *Hay Truck*, given in full in Example 6q. Place your capo at the fifth fret

We begin with a descending bassline on the D and A strings, while the G and the B strings are plucked. The bassline continues to descend in bar two before resolving to the open G shape at the end of the bar. Pay close attention to the fingerpicking directions I have given in the notation to see how I approach playing this sequence.

Example 6n

Example 6o is the main theme to *Hay Truck* and features some wide chord voicings. The bass notes are played on the lower strings while the melody rings clearly on the higher strings. Keep this approach in mind when writing your own fingerstyle arrangements.

Example 6o

If you want to learn one fill from this book to play to impress your friends, I suggest Example 6p. The combination of slides and legato in the G Major scale create an ear-catching fluid texture. While this example is played with a capo, it also works beautifully with an open G Major chord shape.

Example 6p

Example 6q is the full piece *Hay Truck*. If you have worked through the previous examples it will feel much more approachable, so ensure you can play those from memory before tackling this example. As always, listen to the audio a few times to hear the nuances of how I perform this track before playing it yourself.

There are few things I love more than seeing people perform my music all around the world, so do email me or tag me on social media so I can see you playing and help you improve!

Example 6q

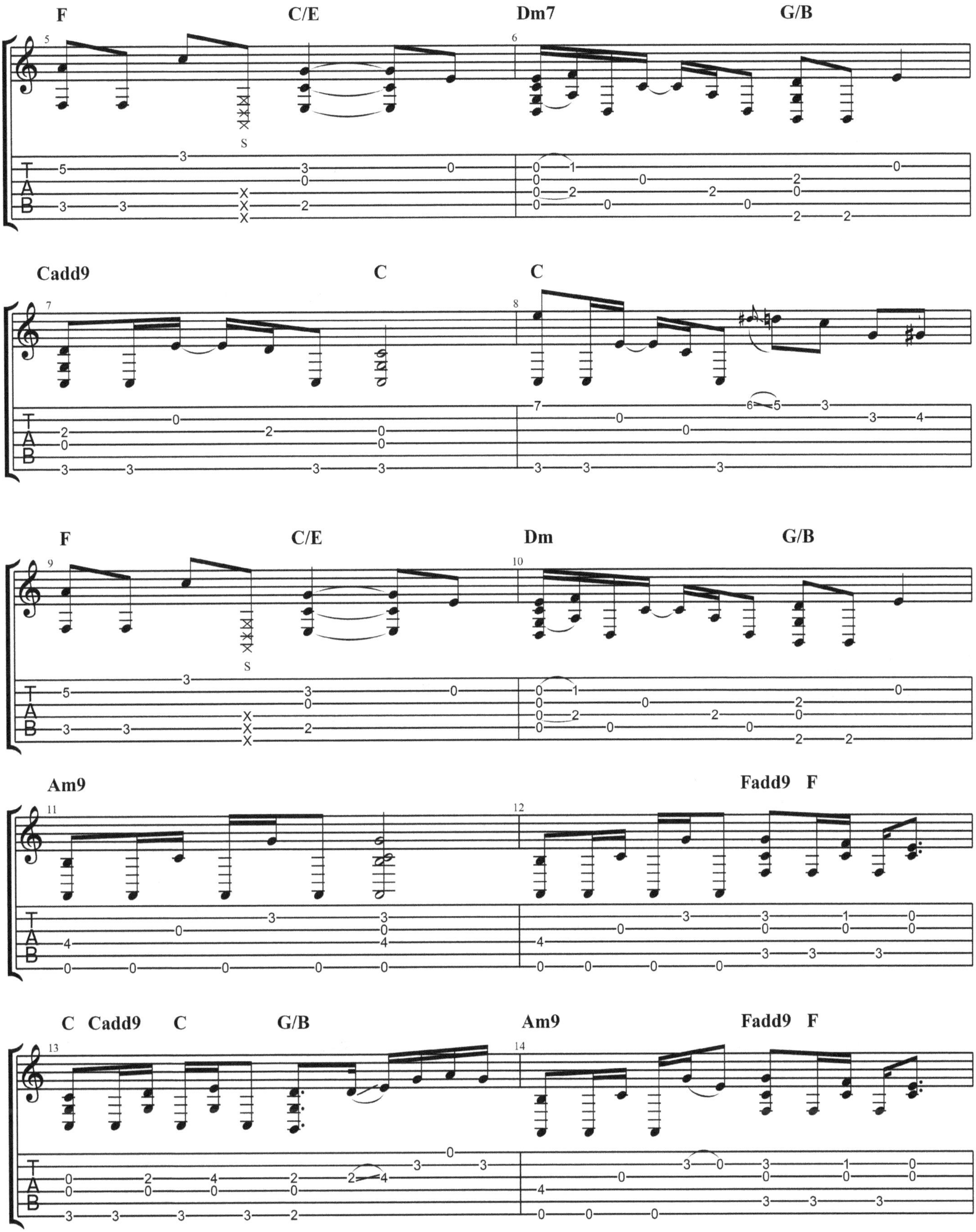
F
C/E
Dm7
G/B
Cadd9
C
C
F
C/E
Dm
G/B
Am9
Fadd9 F
C Cadd9 C
G/B
Am9
Fadd9 F

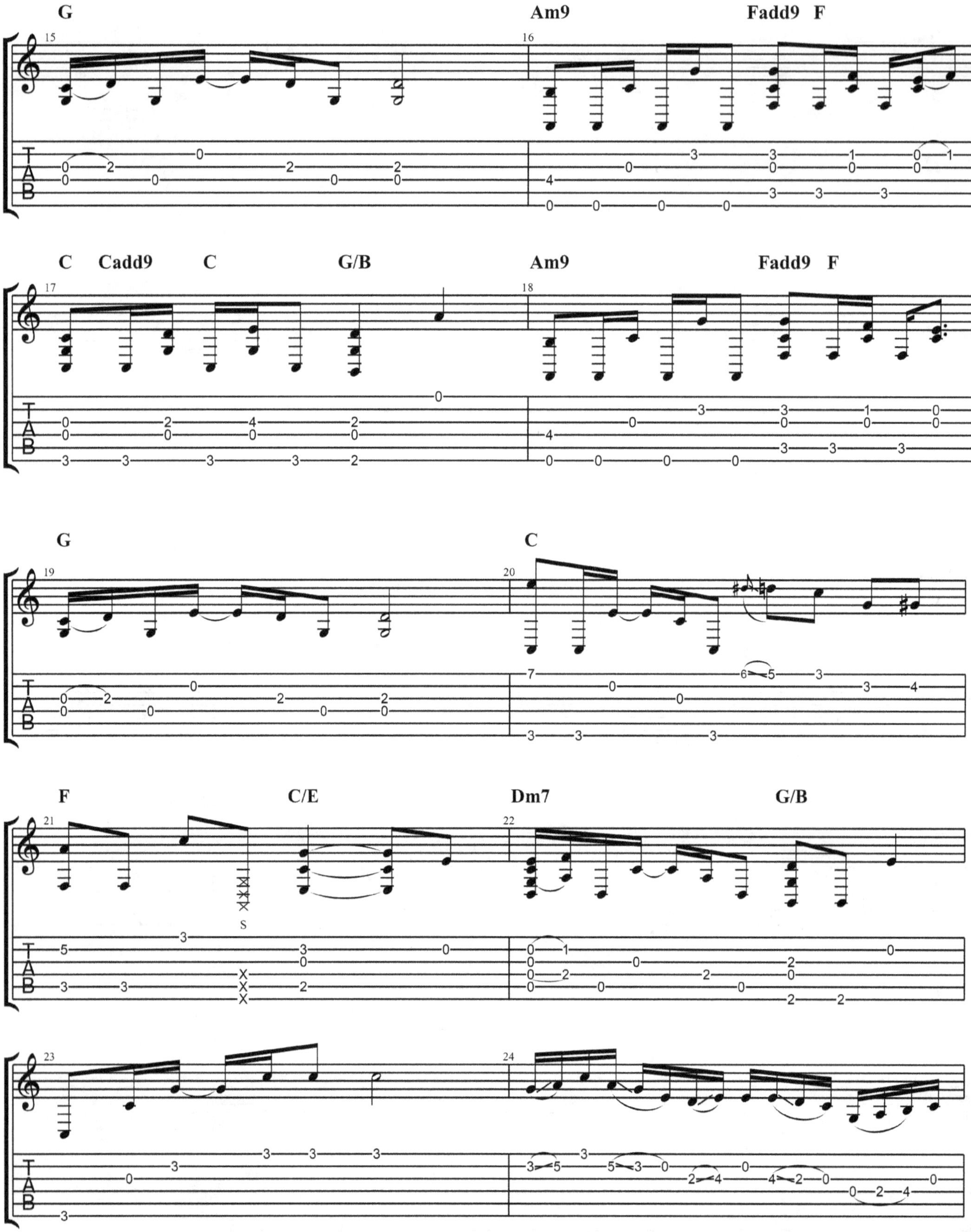
G
Am9
Fadd9 F
C Cadd9 C
G/B
Am9
Fadd9 F
G
C
F
C/E
Dm7
G/B
S

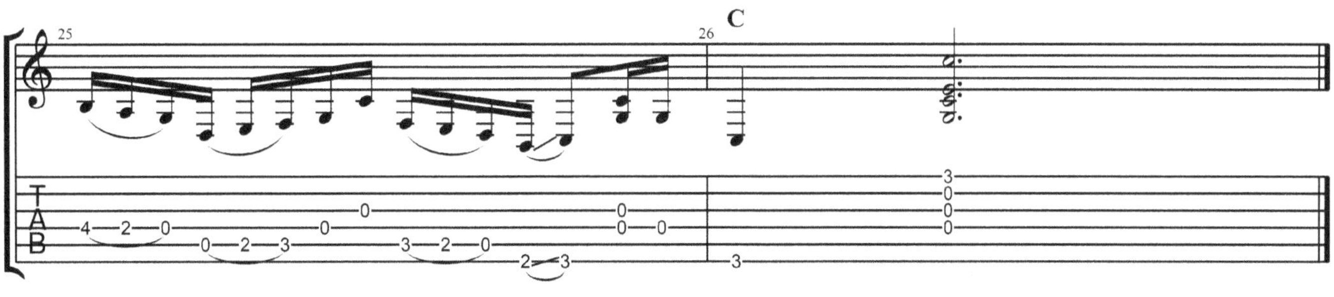
C

Chapter Seven - It's Not Over

Music is both a language and a form of emotional expression. Often, the songs I have written that have come from a place of pain connect to the listener in a far deeper way. *It's Not Over* has proven to be one of those pieces.

The remarkable thing about music is that every key has its own character and nuances. For me, G# Minor is one of the saddest minor keys and in researching this I found the following quote:

Grumbler, wailing lament, difficult struggle; in a word, the colour of this key is everything struggling with difficulty.

Something we've not discussed so far is how emotive fingerstyle guitar playing can be, often to the point of abject soul-stirring. When creating your own fingerstyle arrangements, pay attention to the key you are using and the mood you are in while writing the track. Sometimes by moving the piece into a different key centre and using a capo, you can completely change its feel. Experiment and see how you get on.

As well as the full piece, I have included a breakdown of some of the crucial licks and techniques used in this song. When playing through the examples use a capo at the fourth fret. The full video of the piece *It's Not Over* can be seen here:

https://www.fundamental-changes.com/creative-fingerstyle-videos/

Example 7a features the main theme which is based around the three chord shapes of E minor (special voicing), Cadd9 and D6add11. Don't be put off by the fancy name of the latter chord, it is literally a C Major chord shape slid up two frets. Look at the chord shapes below to see how they are played.

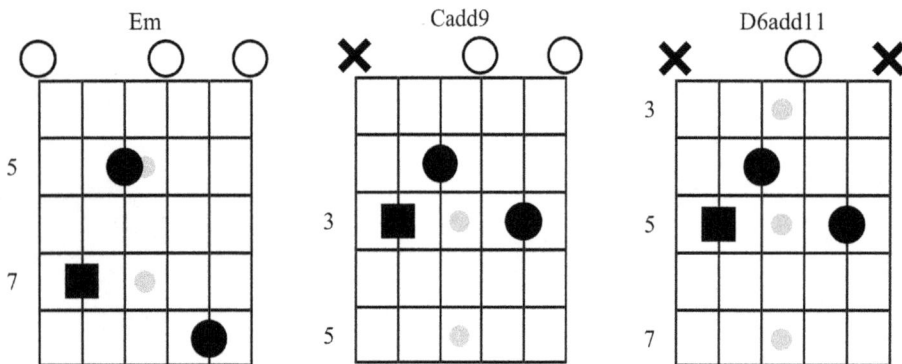

You will notice on the video that for the Cadd9 chord I rake my thumb through the A to the B strings. The other thing to pay close attention to is to let the notes of each chord ring out for as long as possible.

Example 7a

The start of the B section in this piece uses a Gsus2 chord followed by a G Major Pentatonic hammer-on lick. Practice this G Major passage on its own as it's a useful idea to use whenever you are playing progressions around an open G Major shape. The G/B (a G Major chord with a B in the bass) acts as a passing chord to the ringing open CMaj7 voicing. Rake through the CMaj7 chord with your thumb in the same way as you did for the Cadd9 in previous example.

Example 7b

Example 7c shows one of my favourite fills from *It's Not Over*. It starts off around the E Natural Minor scale and descends to the Cadd9 chord shape that features so heavily throughout this piece.

The stand-out part in this lick is the six-note passage in the middle that is played with only one pluck. Break it down into two-note phrases and build them up, block by block. You will find that you need to play both the fifth fret pull-off and the hammer-on back to the 2nd fret with your first finger. Be aware of that adjustment as you practice the phrase.

Example 7c

Now I highlight a descending E Natural Minor legato fill. Watch the video and listen to each audio track individually to see how I perform it.

https://www.fundamental-changes.com/creative-fingerstyle-videos/

Example 7d

Example 7e demonstrates an E Blues scale phrase that covers all six strings using two-positions on the neck. The hardest part of this phrase is the movement from the 7th to the 2nd fret on the G string. I usually play this with my first finger. Although you will have to jump strings from the previous note with the same finger, the rest of the phrase is more comfortable that way. As always, experiment, make it your own, and see what works for you.

Example 7e

The final Emin9 chord of this piece includes some tapped harmonics. Fret the Emin9 chord, then tap on the fret wire exactly 12 frets above each note. As soon as you tap the note, release the tap instantly and you will hear the harmonic. (For the open string notes, tap the edge of the 12th fret then release the tap in the same way).

In sequence, the frets you'll be tapping will be the 12, 14, 16, 12, 15 from the bass to the top string. This effective technique is used by many acoustic giants.

Example 7f

There is a lot going on in this piece, but I can honestly say it will be well worth your effort. I've already broken down some of the major components, but there are a few standout parts you should be aware of.

- Bar 18: The G Major Pentatonic fill using slides to move between two different positions on the fretboard

- Bar 22: A smooth G Major Blues scale fill on the high B and E strings

- Bar 24: Two gorgeous voicings of D7add13 and Ebdim7. I use this combination of chords to add tension and release as they resolve to the E Minor chord that follows

- Bars 28-29: This chord run is an extension of the one seen in bar twenty-four and incorporates a C13 with a slide into a Gbdim7. Check out the neck diagrams below for these shapes

- Bar 32: This bar features a lovely low F6/9 chord that holds the suspense before the epic E Blues scale run you learnt earlier

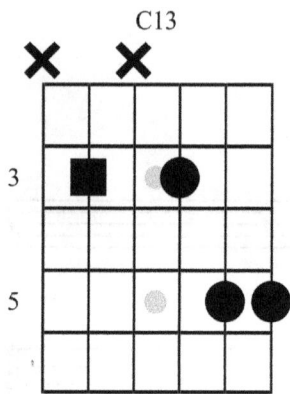

C13

Gbdim7

Example 7g

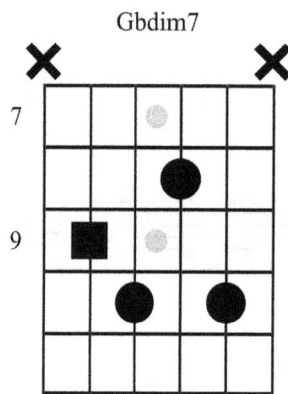

$\quad = 84$

Em

Capo fret 4

Cadd9   D6add11

let ring - ¬   *let ring* - - - - ¬   *let ring* - - - - - - - - - - - ¬

Em

Cadd9   Dadd9add11

let ring - ¬   *let ring* - - - - ¬   *let ring* - - - - - - - - - - - ¬

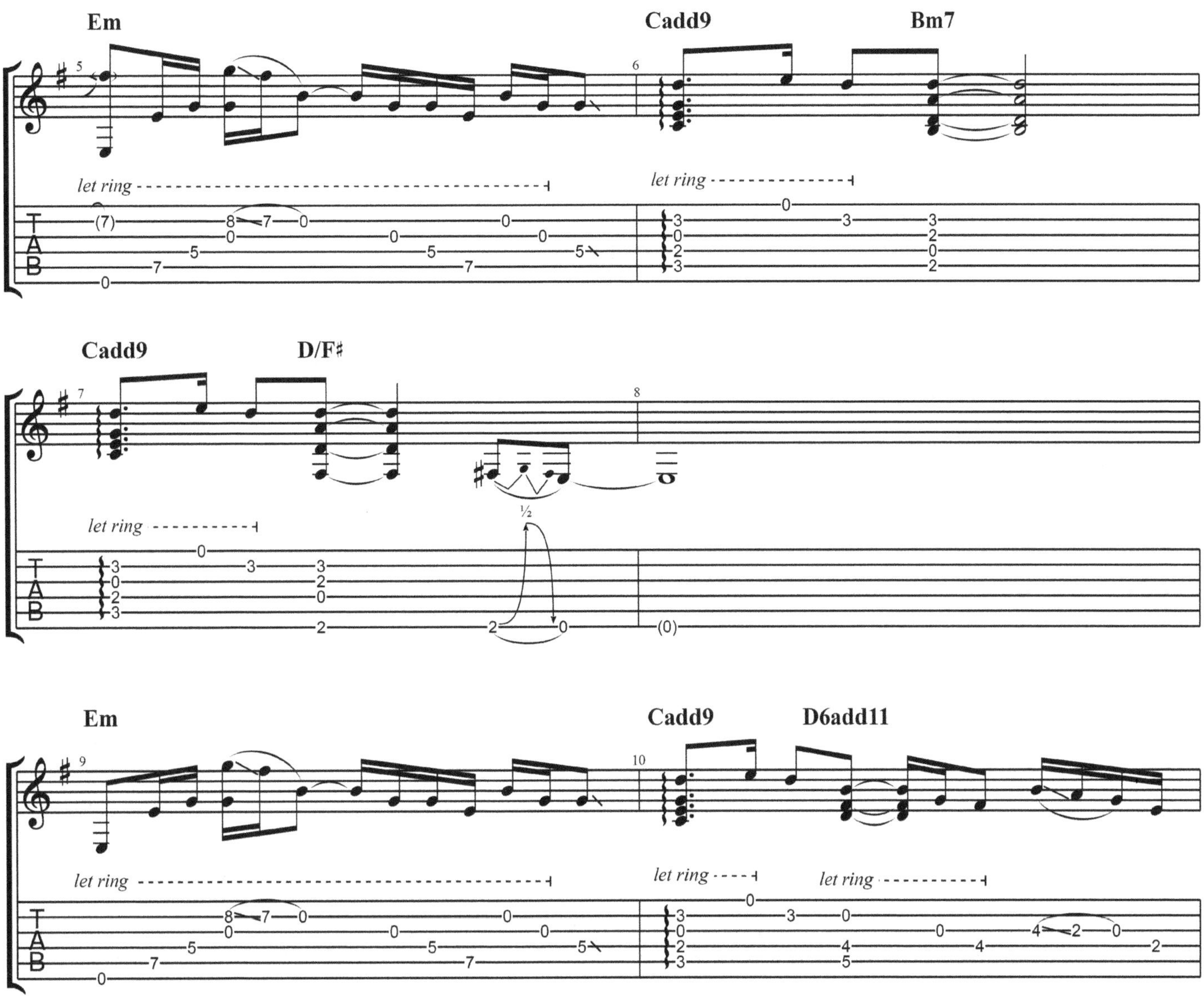
Em
Cadd9
Bm7
let ring
let ring
TAB
Cadd9
D/F♯
let ring
½
TAB
Em
Cadd9
D6add11
let ring
let ring
let ring
TAB

Em
Cadd9
Dadd9add11
let ring
let ring
let ring
Em
Cadd9
Bm7
let ring
let ring
Cadd9
D/F♯
let ring
½
Gsus2
G/B
Cmaj7
let ring

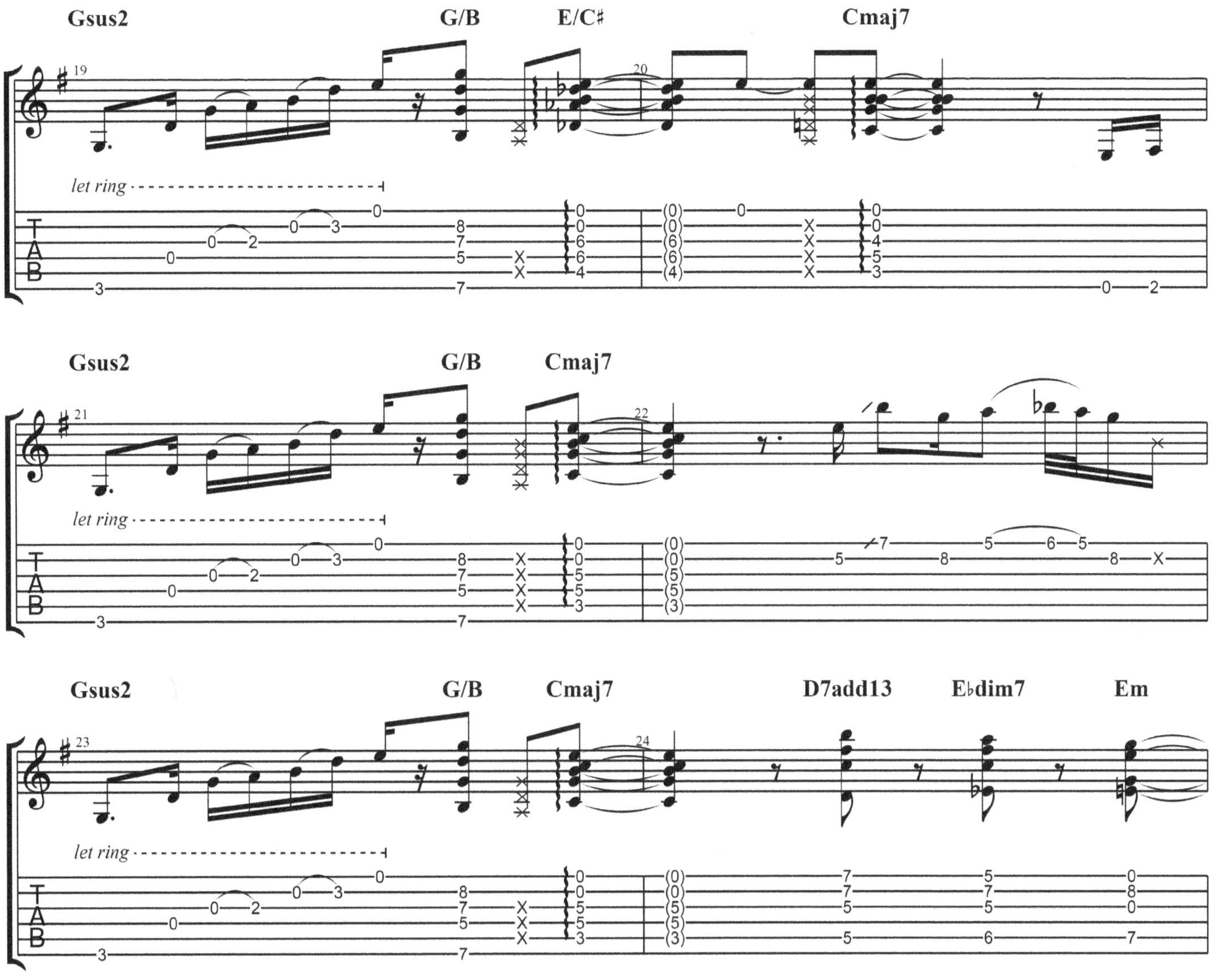
Gsus2
G/B
E/C♯
Cmaj7
let ring
Gsus2
G/B
Cmaj7
let ring
Gsus2
G/B
Cmaj7
D7add13
E♭dim7
Em
let ring

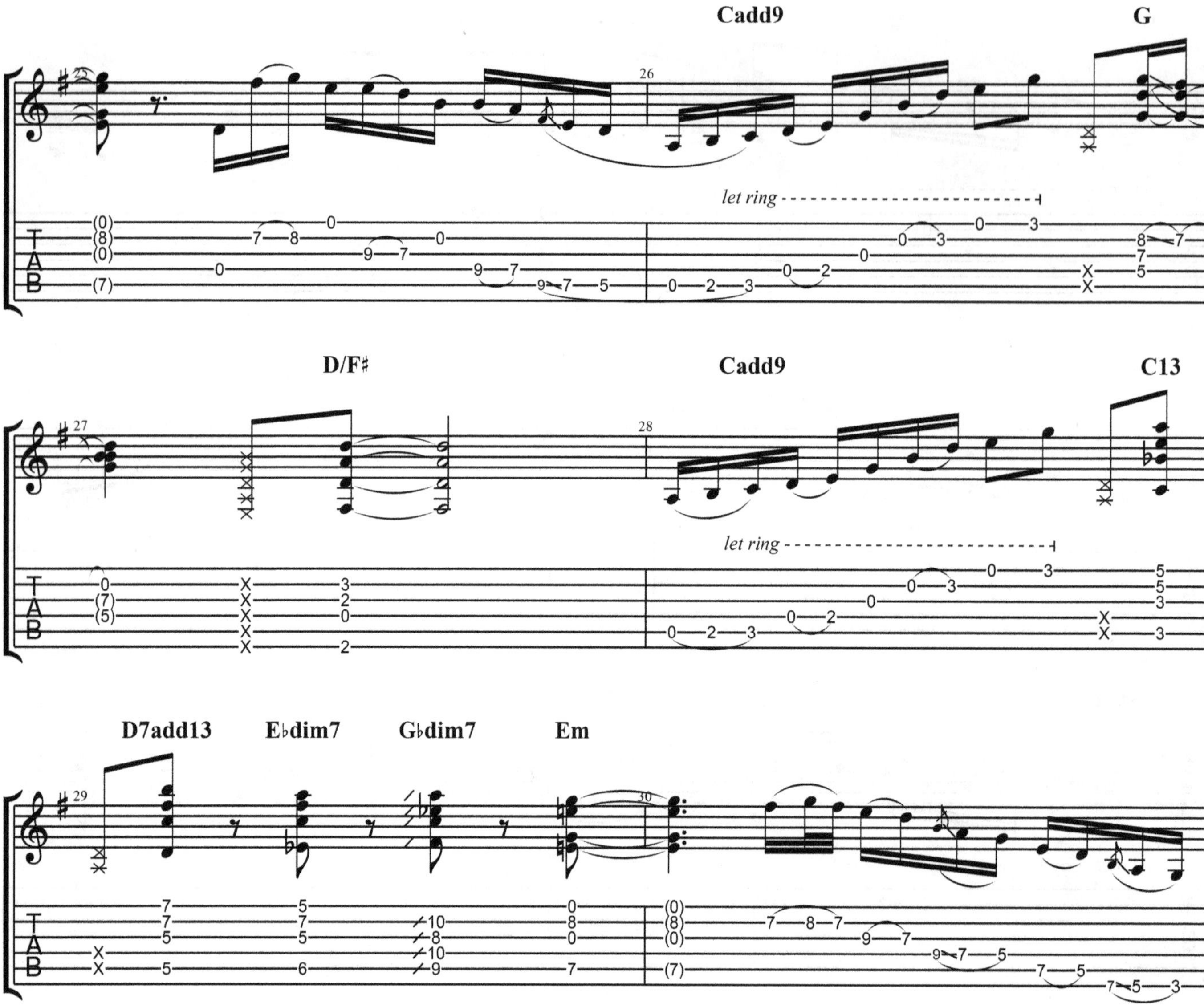
Cadd9
G
let ring
D/F♯
Cadd9
C13
let ring
D7add13
E♭dim7
G♭dim7
Em

Cadd9
G
D/F♯
F6/9
let ring
Em
Cadd9
D6add11
let ring
let ring
let ring
Em
Cadd9
Dadd9add11
let ring
let ring
let ring

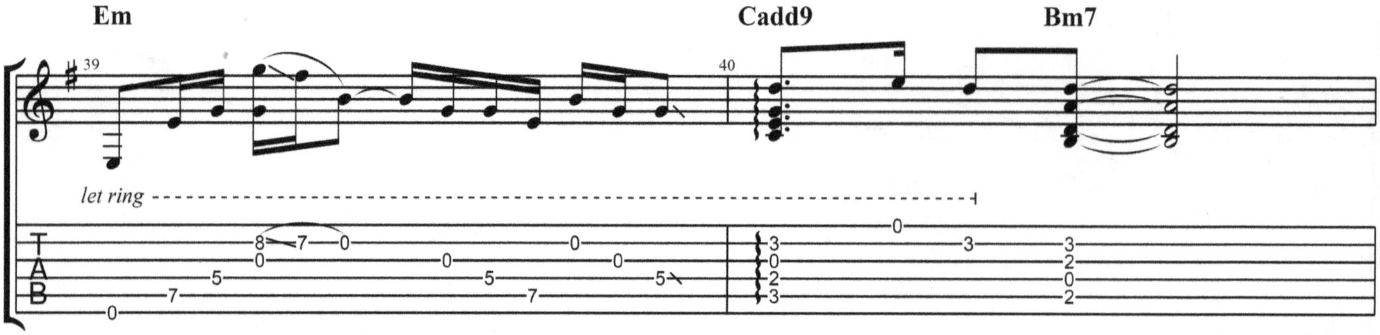
Em
Cadd9
Bm7
39
40
let ring
T
A
B

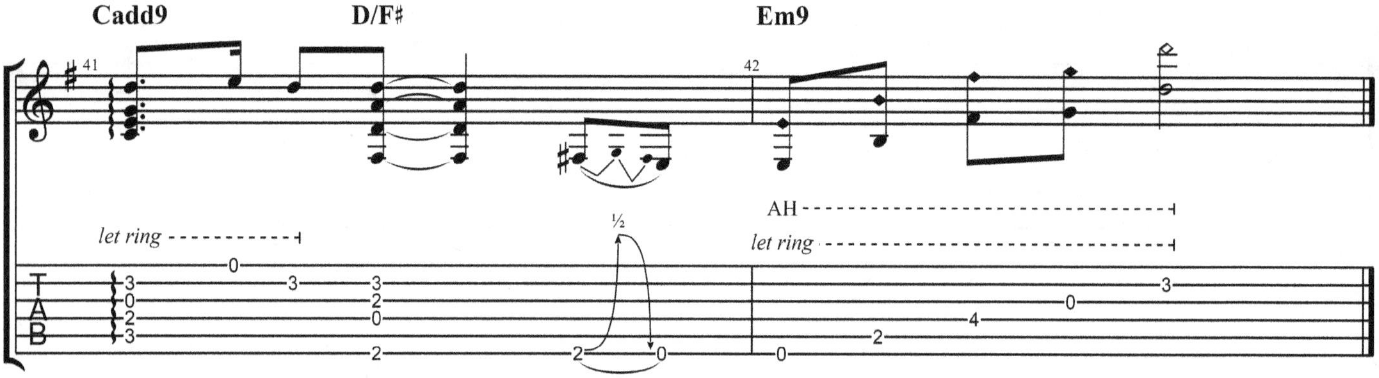
Cadd9
D/F♯
Em9
41
42
let ring
AH
½
let ring
T
A
B

Chapter Eight - GCC

This piece was written as background music for a project at a local church called Guildford Community Church (GCC). I wanted to use lots of open chords and have a super melodic upbeat melody, retaining some of the popular aspects of modern worship guitar playing, while adding my own fingerstyle sound to it. You will notice that I prefer using a capo at the third or fourth fret, as this is where I have found the sweet spot to be on my acoustic guitars. This piece uses one at the third fret.

The melody is the focal point of the piece and provides its foundation. I am confident that after just one listen you will be able to hum the melody line. As mentioned before, the most popular songs you write will generally be the most melodic.

One important takeaway of this piece are the fills that come between each open chord. Being able to spice up a simple chord progression this way is both fun and really keeps the listener engaged. So, don't just learn the piece, rip it into bite-size chunks of fills and ideas that you enjoy then write them into your guitar journal.

As with the previous full pieces, I'll dissect a few of the key elements of the track in individual examples before giving the full piece in Example 8d.

Check out the video of me playing the track as well as the individual audio examples as you go through the chapter.

The full video of the piece GCC can be seen here:

https://www.fundamental-changes.com/creative-fingerstyle-videos/

The main melody is based around the chord sequence C, G, Am7, G, then C, G and Csus4. The fills used between these chords are taken from the C Major scale and combine slides and legato to form a smooth melody line. You can see the C Major scale mapped across the fretboard below.

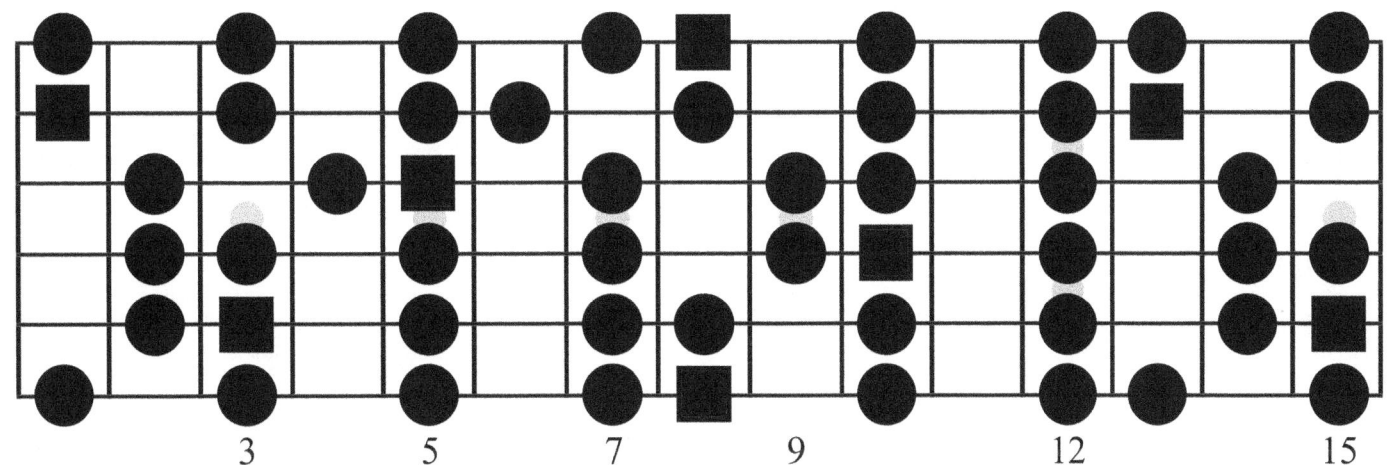

The percussive slaps throughout actually act as part of the main theme, so be sure to play them loud and proud! If you need a reminder of how to perform these refer to Chapter Two.

I have not included fingerpicking directions in this chapter because there are so many notes happening simultaneously it makes the notation look messy. Watch the performance video to see how I pick each note or find a way that suits your own playing style.

Example 8a

When I started teaching this piece many years ago, there was one particular fill that was extremely popular and I've highlighted it below. It's based around an A Blues scale and, when played at a good tempo, it sounds fluid and is quite ear-catching.

One thing to take away from this example is how I use string skipping within the lick. When you are writing and creating your own fills and licks, try adding wider intervallic gaps – don't just always play on adjacent strings.

Example 8b

The breakdown section features a looped chord progression of Dm, G/B, Am and D/F# with a few notes from the A Natural Minor scale played around the A minor chord. See the A Natural Minor scale neck diagram below.

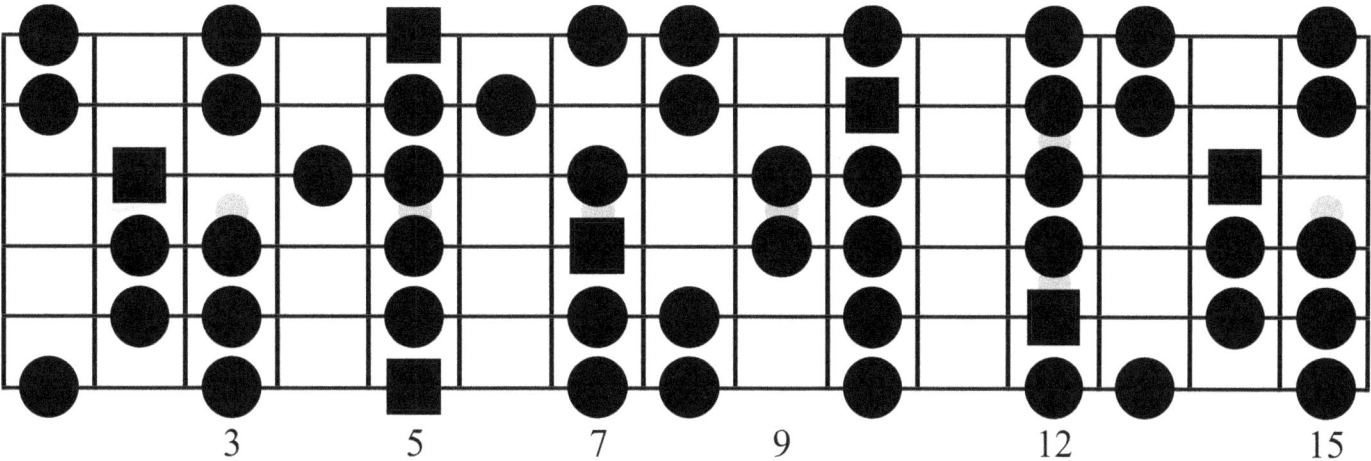

Example 8c

Now it's time to dive into the full piece! Some of the most crucial elements of this piece have already been discussed in the previous examples but below are a few more pointers to look out for when playing this track.

- Bar 12: This chord sequence of F6, Em7, Dm7, C, D, C is a fun way change chord on every melody note

- Bars 13-15: The other main chord sequence used in the piece is Am7, G/B, C and Fsus2. Play the root note of Fsus2 on the 6th string with your thumb, so you keep a finger free to perform the hammer-on later in the bar

The full video of the piece GCC can be seen here:

https://www.fundamental-changes.com/creative-fingerstyle-videos/

Example 8d

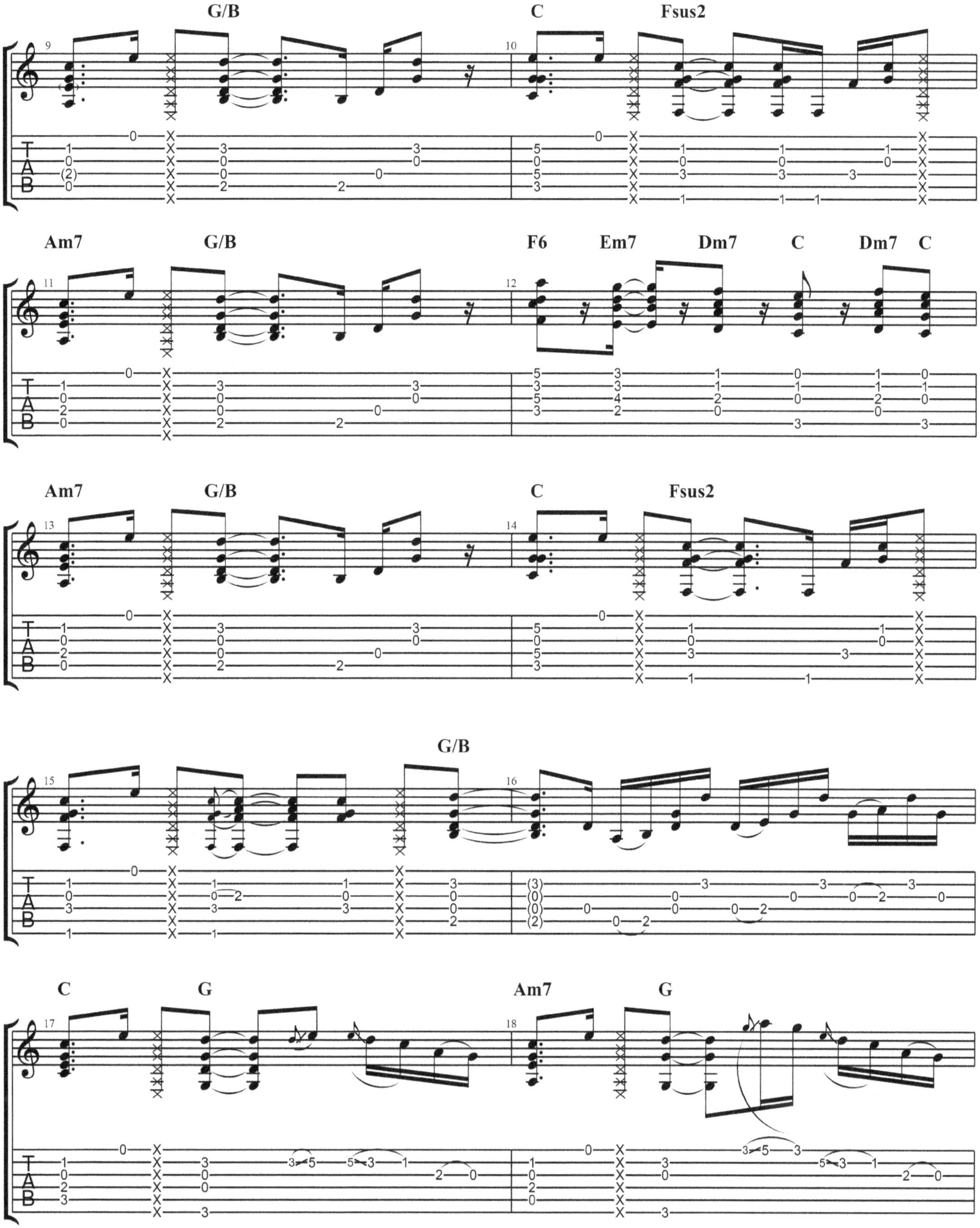
G/B
C
Fsus2
Am7
G/B
F6
Em7
Dm7
C
Dm7
C
Am7
G/B
C
Fsus2
G/B
C
G
Am7
G

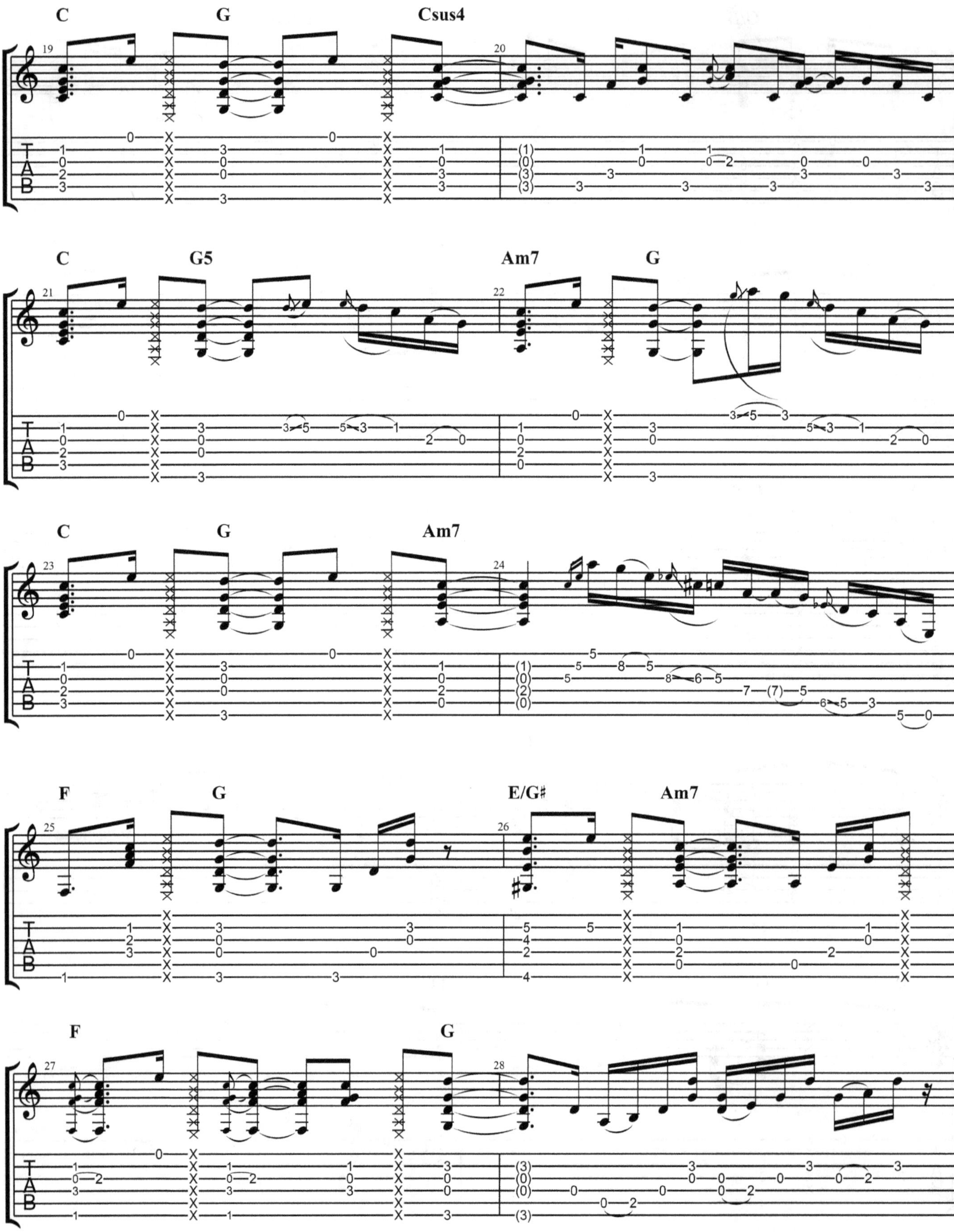
C
G
Csus4
C
G5
Am7
G
C
G
Am7
F
G
E/G♯
Am7
F
G
T
A
B

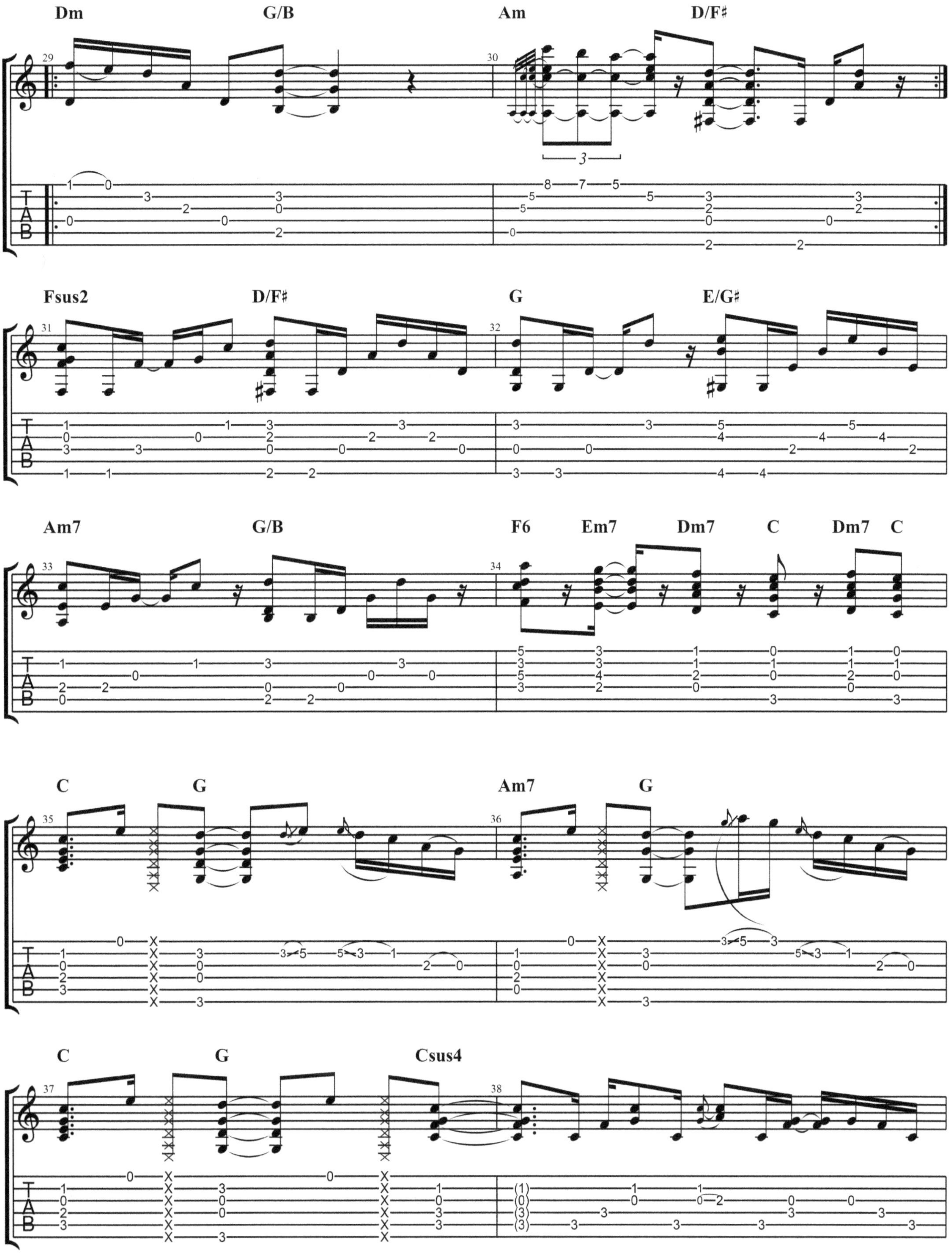
Dm G/B Am D/F♯
Fsus2 D/F♯ G E/G♯
Am7 G/B F6 Em7 Dm7 C Dm7 C
C G Am7 G
C G Csus4

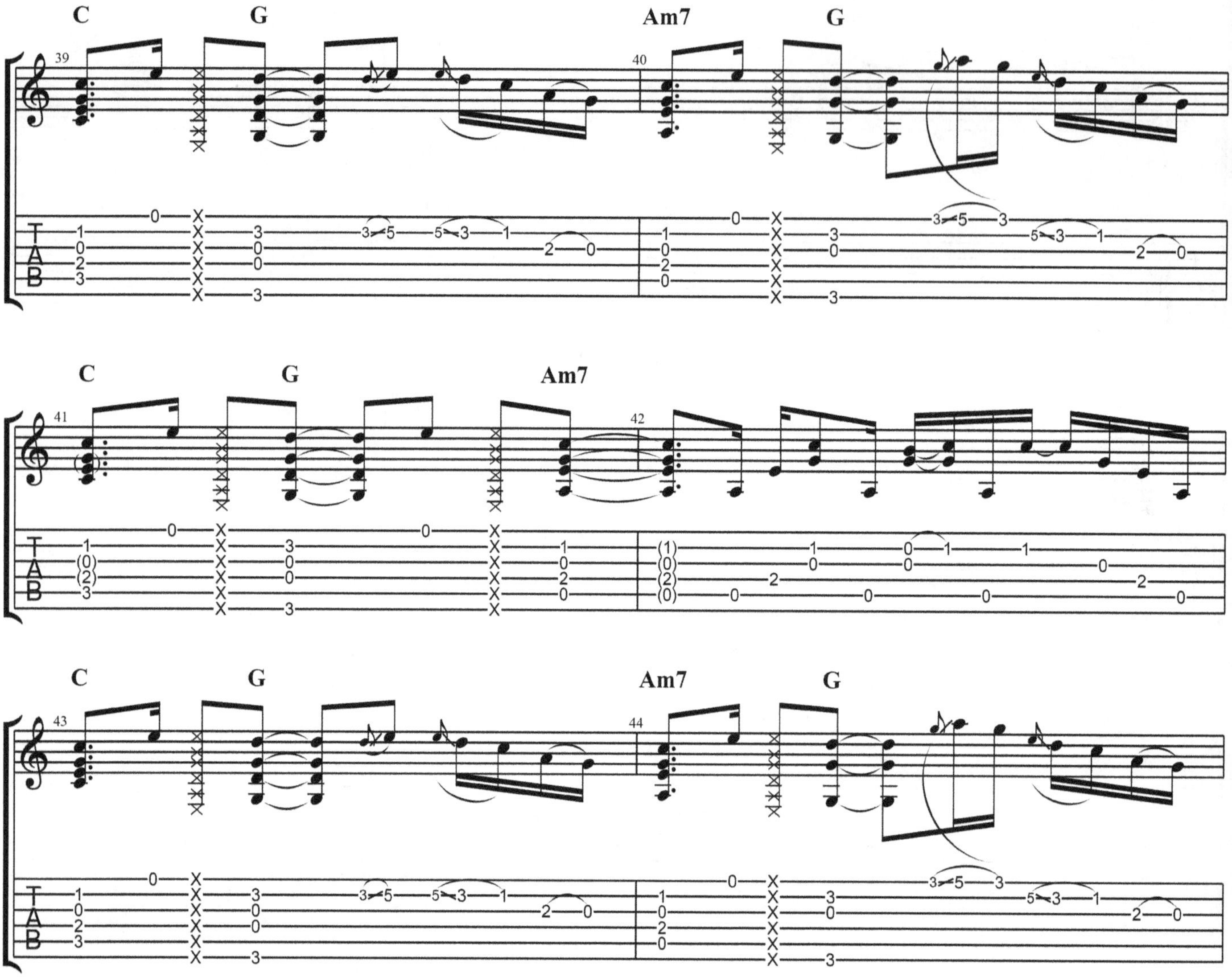
C
G
Am7
G
39
40
T
A
B
C
G
Am7
41
42
C
G
Am7
G
43
44

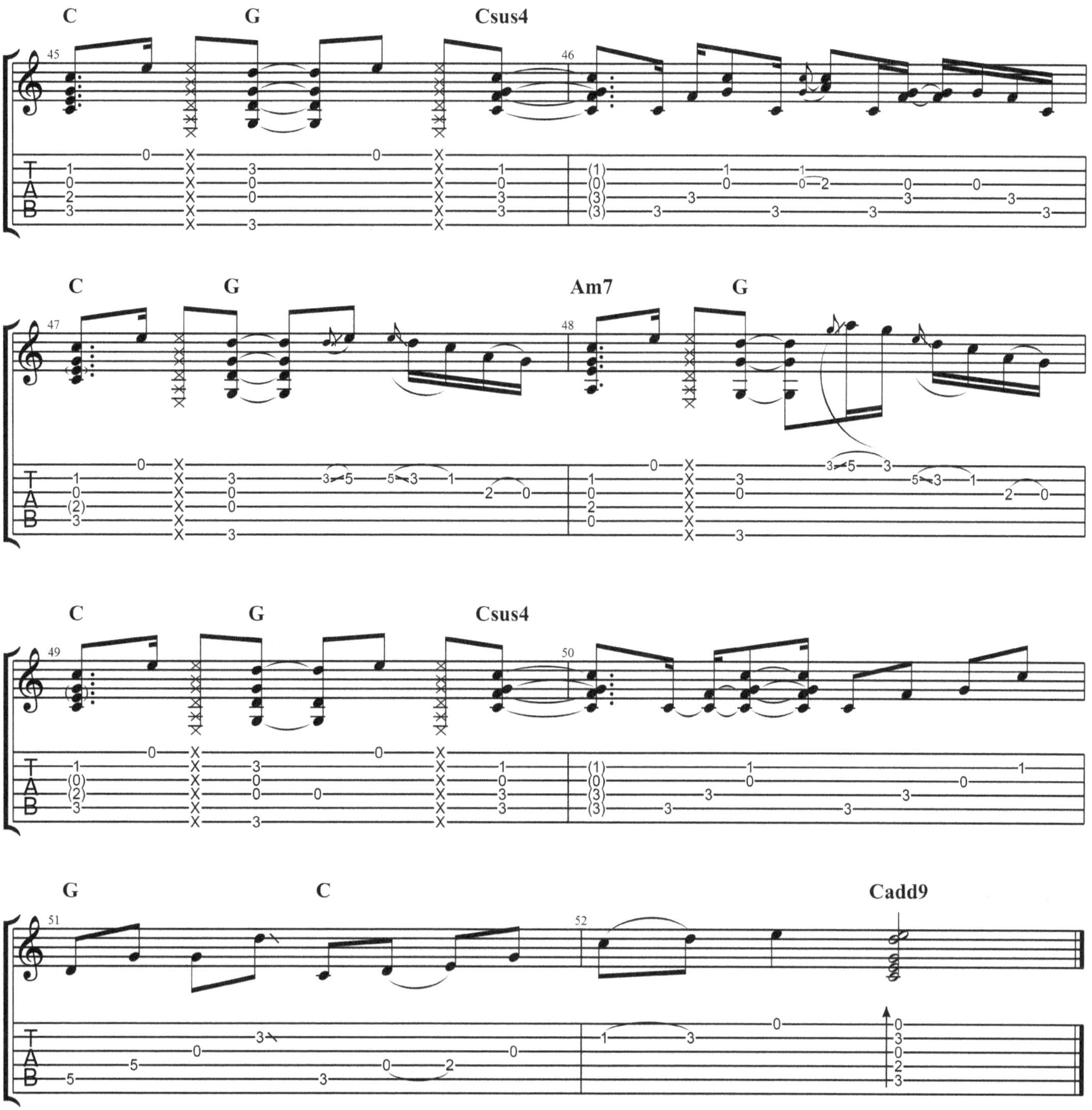
C
G
Csus4
C
G
Am7
G
C
G
Csus4
G
C
Cadd9

Chapter Nine - Drop D Tuning

Drop D is a popular way to tune the guitar whereby the 6th (thickest) E string is tuned down one tone to the note D. It is particularly popular in rock and metal genres, but is also a beautiful tuning to use as an acoustic fingerstyle player.

This chapter includes some of my favourite ideas in drop D tuning and ends with a ballad entitled *Wilderness*.

To begin, get in tune. You can use a tuner for this task, but it's very quick to pick the open D (4th) string and let it ring out, then tune the 6th string down until it's the same pitch an octave below.

Check out the masterpiece *Tears for Jerusalem* by Tommy Emmanuel, which demonstrates Drop D tuning beautifully.

The first thing I want to introduce you to is the concept of a *drone* note. A drone is a note that rings out under, or over, every other note you play in a phrase. Drones are often found in Eastern music but are also commonly heard in fingerstyle pieces too. Drop D acts as a great starting point for drones, and as you can imagine, allows a lot of progressions to be written in the keys of D Major or D Minor.

Suspended chords work particularly well with drone notes. Example 9a explores this idea with a Dsus4 and Dsus2 chords.

Example 9a

I first started to explore music in Drop D tuning after hearing Tommy Emmanuel's *Angelina*. The next example is written in that style and contains a moving bassline of D, F#, G, B, A and fills the gaps with chord voicings. Although you are probably familiar with D/F# and G chords in standard tuning, notice the differences in the shapes now that you're in Drop D.

Example 9b

When I approach a new tuning I like to learn some fundamental chord progressions that will act as building blocks of songs at a later stage. Example 9c shows a B minor, G, D, A progression with the B string open on each chord to create an open, ringing texture.

Example 9c

I first fell in love with the sus2 chord sound when listening to the song *Don't Dream It's Over* by Crowded House. It lends itself beautifully to solo guitar tunes, so keep that in mind when writing your own music.

Example 9d

Now I want to show you some of the essential components you can use when creating your own fingerstyle compositions. We'll apply some of these ideas to the Drop D piece at the end of the chapter.

The first thing I find hugely beneficial is using sixth intervals. Sixths can be played in a number of ways on the guitar but are normally played on non-adjacent strings. Example 9f shows a D Major scale played in sixths on the D and the B strings.

Example 9e

Example 9f uses the D Major scale in sixths and builds them into a chord sequence around D, B minor and A. You can experiment by letting the open D string ring on the D Major chords or hold it for just one beat. Notice the suggested chord fingerings.

Example 9f

Example 9g demonstrates how to play the D Natural Minor scale in sixths on the D and the B strings.

Example 9g

Now here's the minor equivalent of Example 9f using the minor sixth shapes from the previous example.

Example 9h

The next example shows how to create D Major scale sixth shapes on the G and E strings.

Example 9i

Example 9j takes advantage of the droning low D string throughout and also uses the open B string as a pedal-tone note between sixth shapes.

Example 9j

This example shows D Natural Minor scale sixth shapes on the G and E strings.

Example 9k

The following examples are chunks of the final piece of this chapter, *Scarcity*, written in Drop D. Work your way through them sequentially so that the final piece will feel easier and more familiar.

Here's the introduction to *Scarcity* which uses a combination of natural harmonics and a droning low D note to set the stage for this dark-sounding track.

Example 9l

The first part of the melody uses the D Major scale and combines hammer-ons and a slide to create a flowing legato texture.

Example 9m

This example highlights the use of sixths in D Major before arriving at a beautiful Em9 chord shape.

Example 9n

This lick is a real crowd pleaser when played at full tempo. The underlying chord progression is E minor to G, but I start off with the power chord shapes before decorating the legato patterns with hammer-ons, pull-offs and slides. The lick finishes with some more sixth shapes on the G and E strings. Learn the lick in small chunks before piecing them together.

Example 9o

Cascading scales can help you to break away from predictable box-shape patterns. The simple principle is to play any note from the scale on an open string if you can. Here's one way to create a descending D Major scale pattern using the cascading scale approach.

Example 9p

Example 9q shows *Scarcity* in its entirety. This piece is played freely, and I wasn't sticking to a strict tempo when recording it.

Take the elements you enjoy from this and keep them in your guitar journal. I recommend that you add audio and video recordings to your guitar journal to track your progress and give quick access to your ideas. It is also beneficial to date the recordings you create, so that you will have clear evidence of the progress you have made over time.

Example 9q

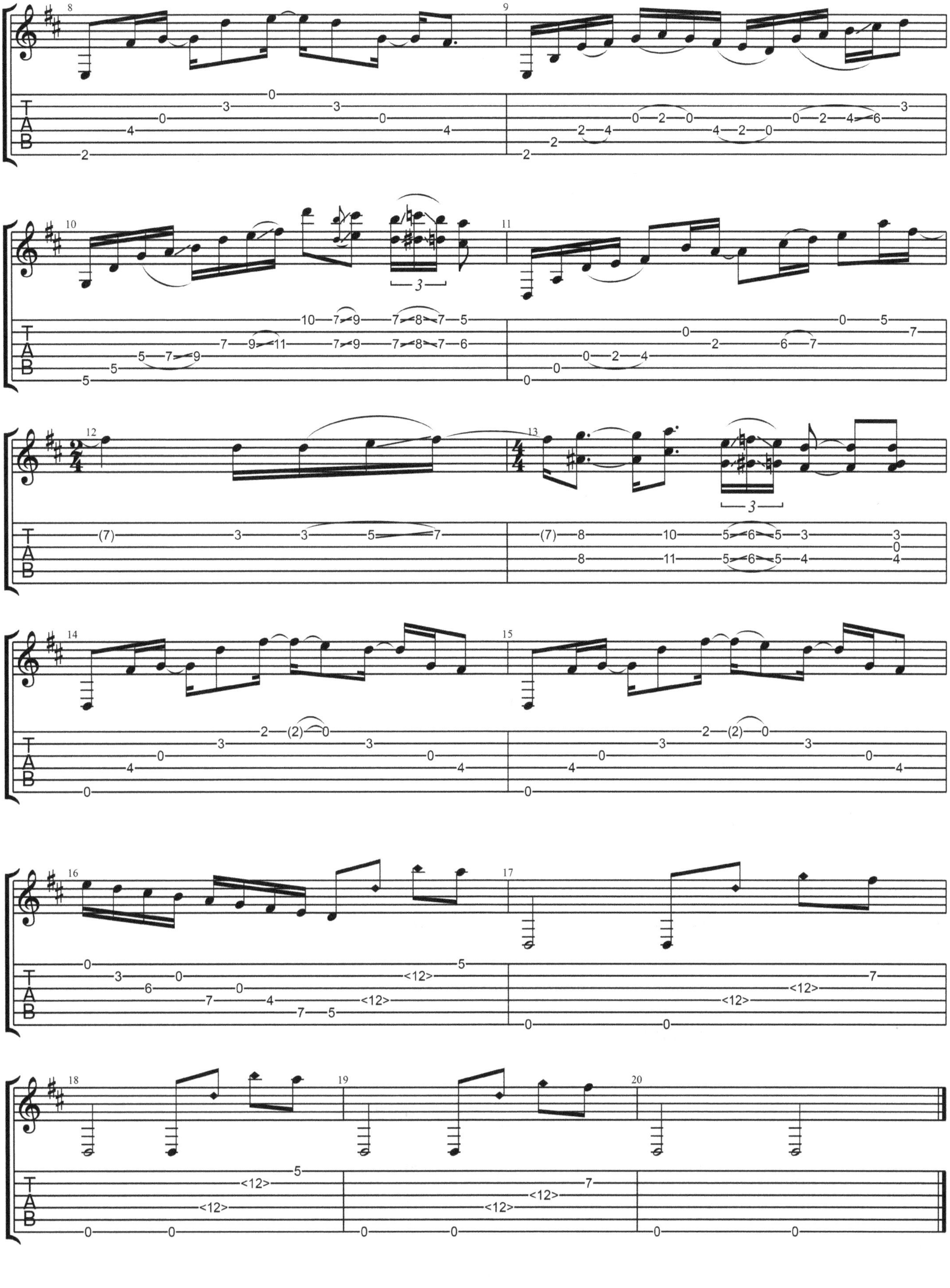

Chapter Ten - Belle

Congratulations on getting this far! I know the amount of practice and study that it's taken.

All the pieces in this book are extremely personal and dear to me. One from my dad, one written to a friend, and some composed from a broken place. I wanted to include them to show you the depth and levels of emotion and expression that can be achieved using the fingerstyle technique. This chapter's piece was written years ago for a close friend of mine. When you have a name that literally translates as "beautiful", it puts a bit of pressure on you to write something that lives up to the name!

Belle contains three major parts, all built around ringing chord voicings. I've written many of these chords as grid shapes as I feel these are worthy of extra study. Highlight your favourite chords from this piece and add them to your journal. The first thing to do when you learn a new chord shape is to try to immediately write a riff or a lick based around it. This helps you to memorise the new shape in a practical, musical way.

I'll begin by breaking down some of the main ideas of this piece into isolated examples before giving the full piece at the end of the chapter.

Watch the video lesson below before working on the examples, so you know what you're aiming for. I go into detail about the construction of the track and the techniques involved.

https://www.fundamental-changes.com/creative-fingerstyle-videos/

To begin with, tune to Drop D and place a capo at the 3rd fret.

Chord shapes, fills and percussive slaps are the major feature of the main melody. First fingerpick through the shapes on their own, and when they become comfortable add in the extra decorations. The chord shapes are written for you below.

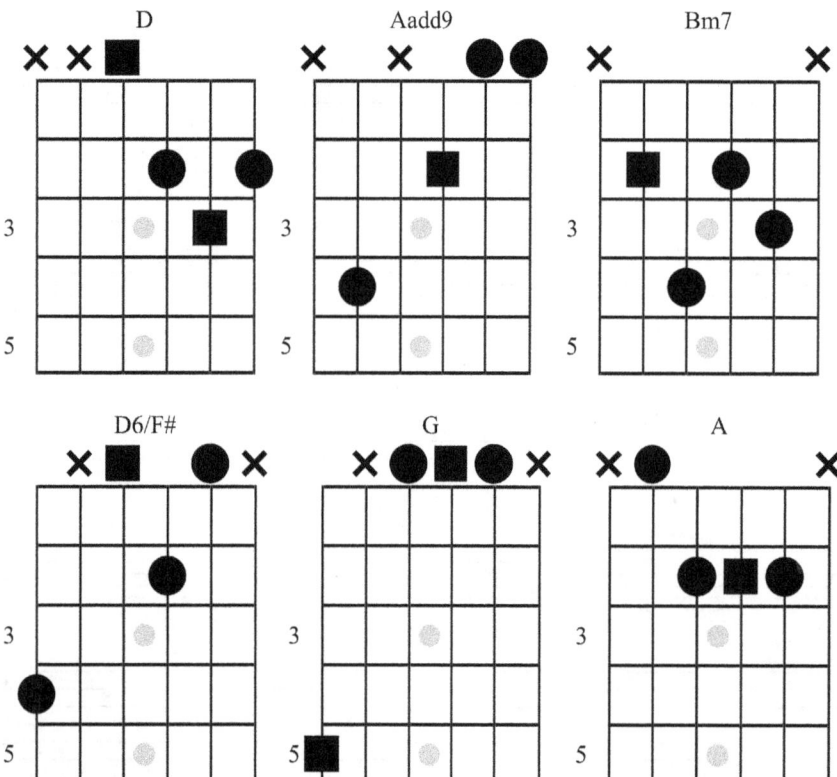

Example 10a

Example 10b is the main theme of the B section. The voicings came about because I wanted the melody to ring on the upper strings. It was a trial and error approach to find the chord voicings that worked underneath. Sometimes, I think musicians make it look like they have perfect inspiration when writing a track, but often it's more of a process. The only rule is that if it sounds good, it is good!

These DMaj13 and C#m7#5 chord voicings might be new to you. Have a look at them in the diagrams featured below.

Example 10b

This example features a descending D Major scale with the B, G and D notes played on open strings. A cool trick is to write out the scale you are using on a piece and identify if any of those notes can be played as an open string. If not, add a capo and see if by moving it around you can access more open string notes in the scale.

Example 10c

Here's the C section to this piece. This part of the track features some wonderful open chord voicings that may be new to you, so the neck diagrams for these shapes are shown below. Let each note run as smoothly into the next as possible.

Example 10d

This run features the E7sus4/A chord shown above, before a lovely D Major legato pattern is played across the upper four strings. I perform this legato run with my first and third fingers, but you can of course experiment and see what works for you.

If you want to develop your coordination, dexterity and strength in all of your fingers, please refer to my book **The Guitar Finger Gym**

Example 10e

The final lick in *Belle* is an extended harp-like D Major scale run that uses open strings before resolving to a hammer-on pattern around the D Major chord.

Example 10f

We made it! The final example of the book is the transcription of the full piece *Belle*.

The full video of the piece and its breakdown can be seen here:

https://www.fundamental-changes.com/creative-fingerstyle-videos/

Example 10g

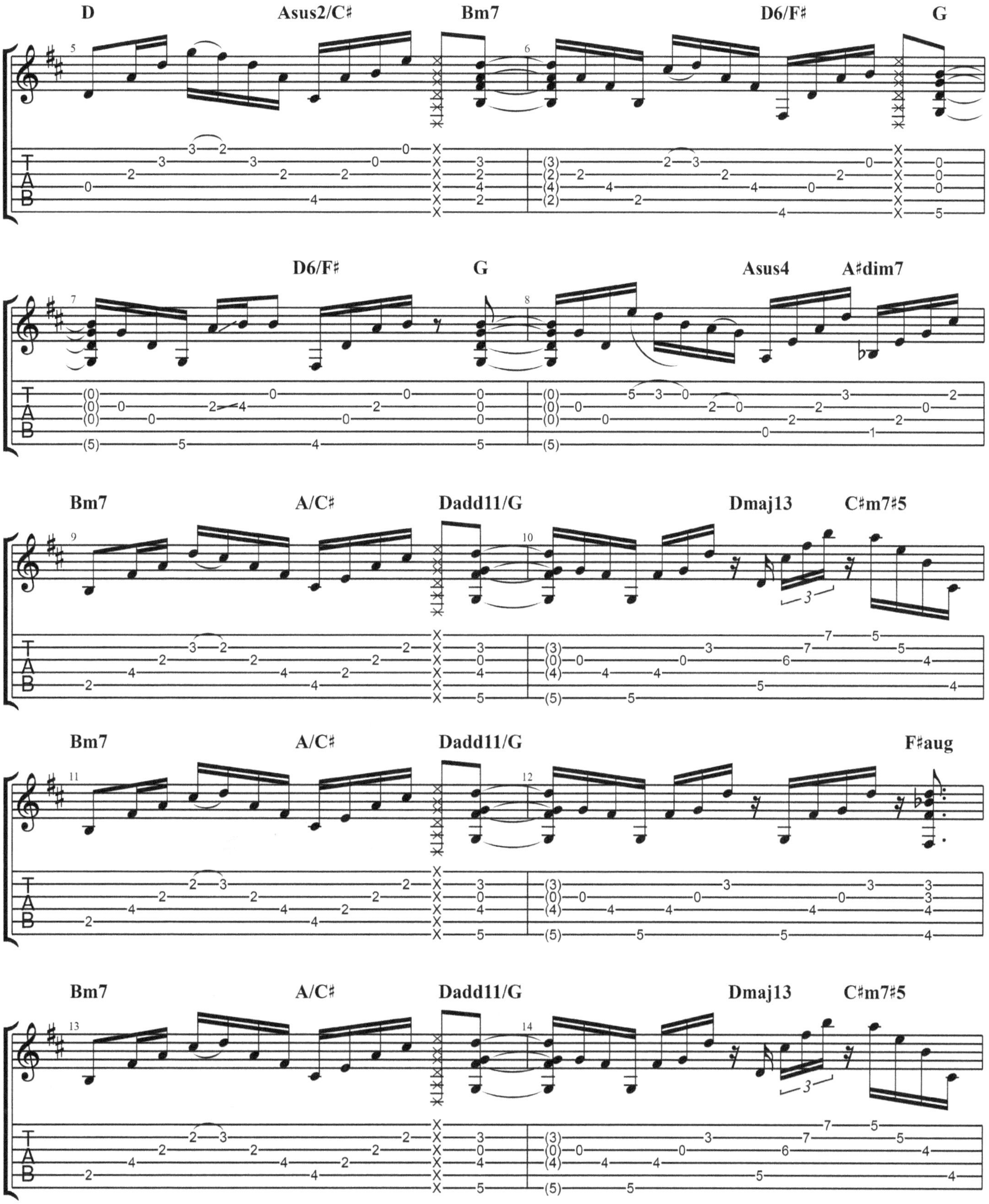
D
Asus2/C♯
Bm7
D6/F♯
G
D6/F♯
G
Asus4
A♯dim7
Bm7
A/C♯
Dadd11/G
Dmaj13
C♯m7♯5
Bm7
A/C♯
Dadd11/G
F♯aug
Bm7
A/C♯
Dadd11/G
Dmaj13
C♯m7♯5

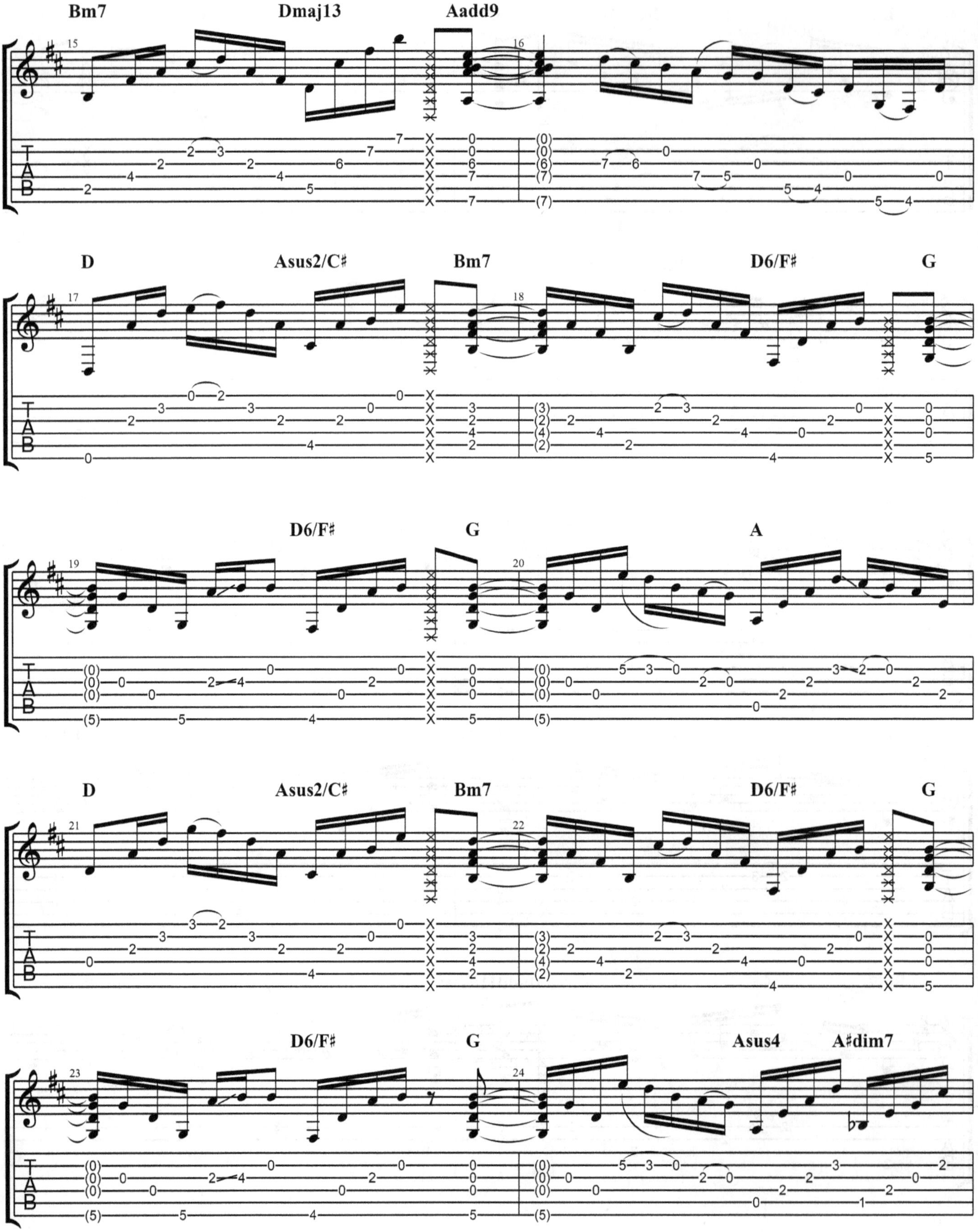
Bm7
Dmaj13
Aadd9
D
Asus2/C♯
Bm7
D6/F♯
G
D6/F♯
G
A
D
Asus2/C♯
Bm7
D6/F♯
G
D6/F♯
G
Asus4
A♯dim7

Bm
A7/C♯
Dadd11
G6add9
Bm
A7/C♯
G6add9
E7sus4/A
D
Asus2/C♯
Bm7
D6/F♯
G
D6/F♯
G
A
D
Asus2/C♯
Bm7

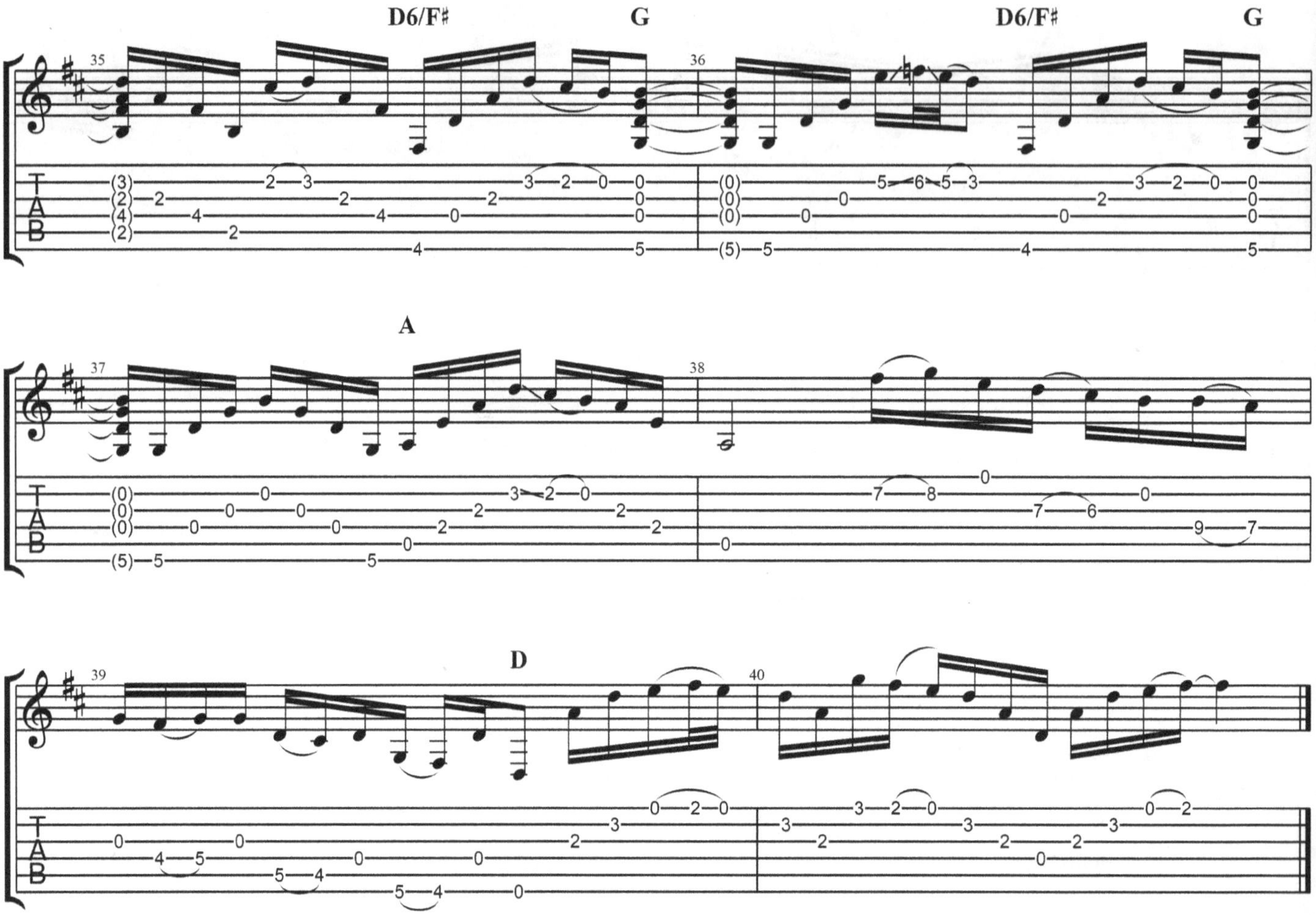
D6/F♯
G
D6/F♯
G
A
D

Conclusion

Congratulations! We've covered a lot of new musical ideas for fingerstyle acoustic guitar and the next step for you is to use the examples in this book as a starting point for creating fingerstyle patterns, phrases and complete songs.

Let your ears guide you. Don't rely too much on the finger patterns and scale shapes that you know to be the "safe" ones. Take a risk. If you play something you don't like, simply don't play it again! Remember the old saying: if it sounds good it is; if it sounds bad, it probably is too.

Remember that there is a difference between practicing and playing. Always practice things you don't know, but make time to play the things you do. This is quite simply the best advice I can give any musician.

An important goal should be to play with other people, so while you are developing your skills in this book, find time to jam with other musicians. Playing with other instrumentalists is the best way to improve your musicianship.

My passion in life is teaching people to play and express themselves through the guitar. If you have any questions, please get in touch and I will do my best to respond as quickly as possible.

You can contact me at **simeypratt@gmail.com** or via our Facebook group **FundamentalGuitar**

Check out my Instagram to see what I am up to in my own playing.

@simeygoesfunkay or my website **www.simonprattguitar.com**

Have fun with your new skills!

Simon